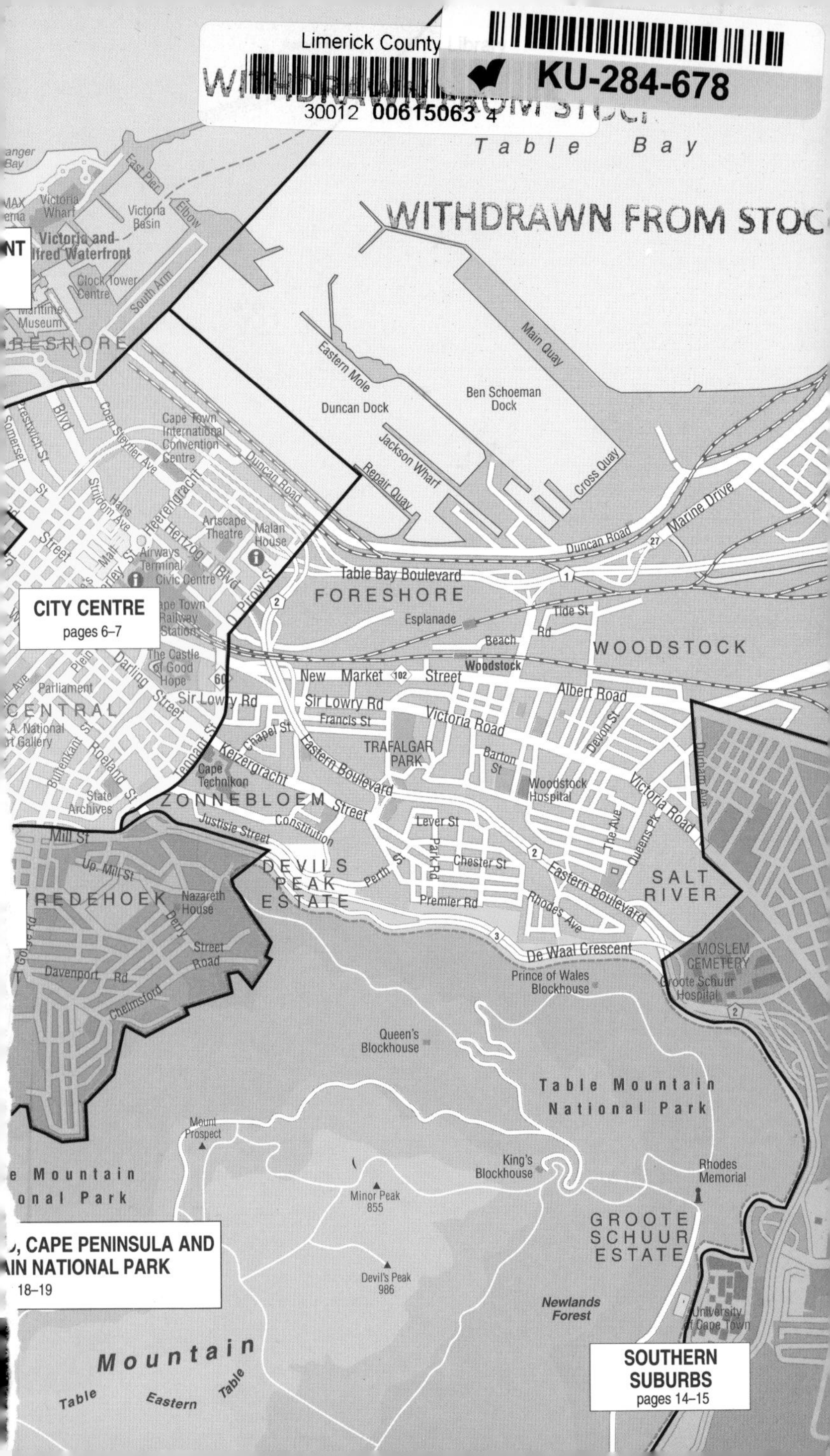
Table Bay
Victoria Wharf
Victoria Basin
East Pier
Elbow
Victoria and Alfred Waterfront
Clock Tower Centre
South Arm
Maritime Museum
Eastern Mole
Duncan Dock
Main Quay
Ben Schoeman Dock
Jackson Wharf
Repair Quay
Cross Quay
Cape Town International Convention Centre
Duncan Road
Coen Steytler Ave
Heerengracht
Hans Strijdom Ave
Artscape Theatre
Malan House
Herzog Blvd
Airways Terminal
Civic Centre
Marine Drive
Duncan Road
Table Bay Boulevard
FORESHORE
Esplanade
Tide St
Beach Rd
WOODSTOCK
CITY CENTRE
pages 6–7
Cape Town Railway Station
The Castle of Good Hope
New Market Street
Woodstock
Albert Road
Parliament
Darling Street
Sir Lowry Rd
Sir Lowry Rd
Francis St
Victoria Road
CENTRAL
S.A. National Art Gallery
Chapel St
Eastern Boulevard
TRAFALGAR PARK
Barton St
Devon St
Keizergracht
Cape Technikon
Woodstock Hospital
Victoria Road
State Archives
ZONNEBLOEM
Street
Justisie Street
Constitution
Lever St
The Ave
Queens Pk
Mill St
Up. Mill St
DEVILS PEAK ESTATE
Perth St
Park Rd
Chester St
Eastern Boulevard
SALT RIVER
Nazareth House
Premier Rd
Rhodes Ave
Street Road
De Waal Crescent
MOSLEM CEMETERY
Davenport Rd
Chelmsford
Prince of Wales Blockhouse
Groote Schuur Hospital
Queen's Blockhouse
Table Mountain National Park
Mount Prospect
King's Blockhouse
Rhodes Memorial
Minor Peak 855
GROOTE SCHUUR ESTATE
Devil's Peak 986
Newlands Forest
University of Cape Town
SOUTHERN SUBURBS
pages 14–15
Mountain
Table
Eastern
Table

CAPE TOWN

smart guide

Discovery CHANNEL

Contents

Areas

Below: Huguenot Memorial Museum, Franschhoek, Cape Winelands.

A–Z

Left: Llandudno, Cape Peninsula.

Below: Helderberg Nature Reserve, Somerset West, Cape Winelands.

Atlas

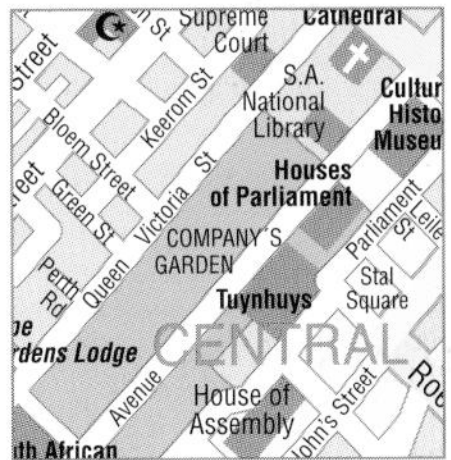

Cape Town

Cape Town, the oldest city in Southern Africa, is regularly heralded as one of the most beautiful on earth. Whether it's the massive sandstone bulk of its iconic Table Mountain, often draped in a flowing 'tablecloth' of clouds, the pristine sandy beaches that line the coastline, the Winelands or the unique flora and fauna, it's everything a traveller could hope for.

Cape Town Facts and Figures

City surface area: **2,500sq km² (967sq miles)**
Population: **2,893,251 (2001 census)**
Time zone: **SAST (GMT+ 2)**
Black Africans: **31.68 percent**
'Coloureds': **48.13 percent**
Whites: **18.75 percent**
Indian/Asian: **1.43 percent**

In the Beginning

Recorded history of the Western Cape does not stretch back much beyond the arrival of European settlers in the 17th century, although the region was populated extensively by the Khoikhoi and the San (known collectively as the Khoisan). While Bartholomew Diaz discovered the Cape of Good Hope in 1488, it was only in 1652, with the arrival of Jan van Riebeeck, that the first European colony was established. The rise of British imperialism in the 18th century soon created conflict with the Dutch settlers in the Cape, as the British began to anglicise the colony. Dutch settlers came under strong pressure to abandon their own language, customs and heritage for English cultural forms and lifestyles, causing many to migrate away from the Cape Colony.

The discovery of gold and diamonds around the turn of the 20th century resulted in rapid industrialisation and urbanisation of South Africa, including the Cape. As a result the black population of South African cities swelled with labourers, and their families lived in informal settlements attached to the cities.

Following rapid urbanisation, many white descendants of the Dutch settlers who had developed a national identity as Afrikaners subsumed themselves into the growing working class. The Nationalist Party came to power in 1948, which rapidly set about formalising the separation of the different racial groups under Apartheid. Whole areas of the city were re-categorised, and many black Capetonians were forcibly removed from their homes. The terms 'Black African', 'Coloured', 'White' and 'Indian' are a legacy of Apartheid but have become part of South African language and are terms commonly used by Capetonians.

It was only in 1990, with the unbanning of the ANC and the release of Nelson Mandela, that South Africa abondoned the policy of Apartheid and moved into a new era of democracy.

The Mother City

Situated in the country's far southwestern corner, Cape Town is a comparatively compact city lying on a narrow peninsula that curls southward into the Atlantic Ocean. Its western and eastern shores are separated by a spinal ridge of mountains, of which Table Mountain is the most dramatic. Fondly referred to as the Mother City, Cape Town is

Right: the majority of Capetonians live in townships around the city.

one of the few cities in the world where Mother Nature rubs shoulders with modern high-rise buildings. It's also a city of cultural contrasts where you can wine and dine in some of the country's best restaurants or take half a day to explore some of the colourful cultures found in the Bo-Kaap and the townships.

City Snapshot

The heart of the city within the breast of the mountain includes the Cape Town Central area, the Central Business District (CBD), surrounding suburbs in the City Bowl, Bo-Kaap and the V&A Waterfront. Moving to the city's outskirts, the Atlantic Seaboard is a haven for beach bums and the wealthy, while the charming fishing village of Hout Bay is where younger families settle. A short drive on the highway, you can head out towards the residential areas south of the city known as the Southern Suburbs, including a winding tour of the Southern Peninsula to Cape Point. Stop in Kalk Bay if you're wanting to trawl antique shops and have lunch at the once-British naval base of Simon's Town, which is also home to a colony of African penguins. Should you grow tired of Cape Town and the Peninsula, hire a car and venture out to the Winelands or the Overberg. Or follow the famous Garden Route through a landscape of coastal fynbos, farmlands and rainforests.

Highlights

▲ **Table Mountain** This dramatic flat-topped, often cloud-covered mountain is alive with indigenous flora and fauna. It towers 1,086 metres (3,563ft) above the city of Cape Town. ▶ **Bo-Kaap** Visit one of the city's oldest areas.

▲ **Cape Point** A tongue of land jutting out into a fierce, stormy ocean littered with ship wrecks. Exceptional coastal views.

▶ **Seals and penguins** Watch seals playing in the harbour and see penguins at Boulders Beach on the Cape Peninsula.

▲ **V&A Waterfront** Home to luxurious shops, live street entertainment and a world-class aquarium. ▶ **Cape Winelands** Discover rolling vineyards, historic architecture, and fine local wines.

City Centre

Once a quiet, sleepy hollow, the City Centre is now rapidly turning into an area alive with diverse heritage, new museums, markets, galleries, good restaurants and a vibey café society. It is relatively small, and can be easily explored on foot. On arrival put on your walking shoes, pick up a map at the Cape Town Tourism office and take to the streets. Many of the interesting spots sit conveniently next to one another along the Museum Mile, and with the lush Company's Garden positioned right in the middle of it all you can easily take a break and laze under the oak trees, people-watch or feed a squirrel or two.

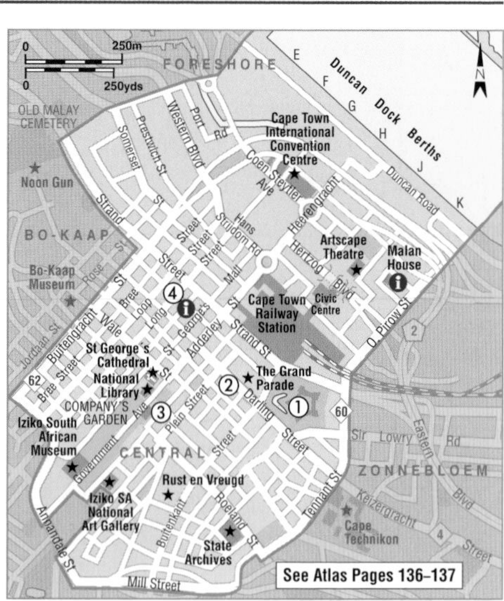

Castle of Good Hope

One of the oldest surviving buildings in South Africa marks the original shoreline, but today the **Castle of Good Hope** ① is surrounded by skyscrapers and modern buildings. Dating back to 1666, this pentagonal fortress is typical of the Dutch defence system adopted in the early 17th century. It has five bastions named after Buren, Leerdam, Oranje, Nassau and Katzenellenbogen – the titles of Prince William of Orange, the Dutch ruler at the time of the settlement – and replaced a simple square fortress built by the Cape's first governor, Jan van Riebeeck. For the first 150 years of colonial rule the Castle of Good Hope was the centre of government and even had dungeons built below sea level. Today the complex functions as a museum and venue for exhibitions and annual events.
SEE ALSO ARCHITECTURE, P.28; MUSEUMS AND GALLERIES, P.76

Left: the Castle of Good Hope.

City Hall

Completed in 1906, the massive **City Hall** ② replaced the Old Town House. This grand sandstone building is typical of the town halls that populated the British Empire. From the building's main balcony Nelson Mandela addressed a 70,000-strong crowd following his release from prison on 1990, the first time he had been seen in

On the corner of Burg and Castle streets is the downtown Tourism Visitor Centre (closed Sat and Sun afternoons), which will gladly give you advice, pamphlets galore and help you plan your visit.

Left: the imposing City Hall.

The Company's Garden has a small tearoom with a shady terrace where you can enjoy an inexpensive lunch, a cake or a cold beer.

public for 27 years. The City Hall houses various municipal offices, the public library and a concert hall which is home to the **Cape Town Philharmonic Orchestra**. Nearby, the **Grand Parade** was once a military parade ground but today it is home to a large market where you will find vegetables, fruit and traditional medicines for sale.
SEE ALSO MUSIC, DANCE AND THEATRE, P.86

Houses of Parliament

At the top of Adderley Street is the leafy entrance to the Avenue, the extension of the Heerengracht (now Adderley Street). To the left you will find the impressive **Houses of Parliament** ③ (enter from the Parliament Street side). This massive building of red brick and tall white pilasters was completed in 1864 and was once the stronghold of white supremacy where many an oppressive law was passed. Watch parliamentary sessions in the National Assembly or take a tour through the debating chambers, library and museum.

Long Street ④

A multicoloured strip of historic Victorian buildings in various states of repair line this famous (some would say infamous) street in Cape Town. It links mountain and sea with a strip of popular bars, delis, restaurants, nightclubs, vintage-clothing boutiques and street-side cafés that hug the bustling sidewalks. It's a street of endless possibilities. Dine out on Asian or African, enjoy an old-fashioned shave at the local barber or take a soak in a Turkish bath at the 100-year-old **Long Street Baths**. Once a year during the **Cape Town Festival**, most bars move their tables and sofas onto the street, art galleries stay open long after dark and the street comes alive with fire dancers, live music and street art. In general, the tone of the street ranges from smart to seedy, so be cautious if you're planning a night out.

Company's Garden

At the heart of the city you'll find the **Company's Garden**, about 6 hectares (15 acres) of which was once the original vegetable garden laid out by the Dutch East India Company. Over time it became a botanical garden. To the north it's overlooked by the **National Library** and to the south beyond formal rose gardens and fountains, you'll find the **Iziko South African Museum** and the **Iziko South African National Gallery**.
SEE ALSO MUSEUMS AND GALLERIES, P.78, 84; PARKS AND RESERVES, P.96

Right: Long Street.

City Bowl

The heart of Cape Town, known as the City Bowl (the 'bowl' created by the flat-topped mountain, flanked by jagged Devil's Peak to the east and the embracing arm of Signal Hill to the west) is a very small area once laid out on a grid system with streets running from south to north and west to east. This makes getting around very straightforward for first-time visitors, and maps are easy to read. The City Bowl is where you'll find some great restaurants and eateries, a cluster of attractive suburbs, as well as access to Table Mountain via the Lower Cable Station.

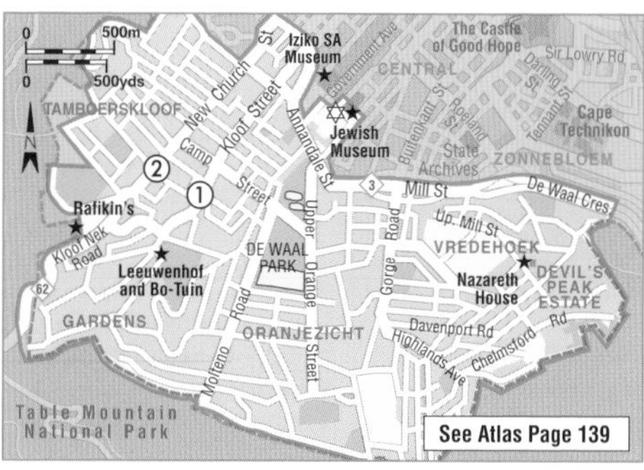

See Atlas Page 139

Kloof Street ①

Kloof Street is Cape Town's creative and culinary hub, also known as the 'Dining Mile'. You'll find a plethora of offbeat, in-vogue cafés and eateries crammed into this narrow street. Creative jet-setters will go wild for the design-book shops, vinyl stores, vintage-clothing boutiques, kitsch collectables and a cutting-edge hair salon where you'll pay a small fortune for a slick hairdo.

If you like looking at venues before deciding where to eat, take a stroll down Kloof Street. Head into Park Road, just off Kloof Street, where you'll be spoilt for choice when it comes to more casual eateries and wine bars.

There's even an art-house cinema called **Labia on Kloof** located on the restaurant strip where they let you take in your glass of wine during the screenings. As you head further up the street, towards the top there are more Asian-themed bars and restaurants as well as a selection of chic décor shops with wonderful locally made contemporary furniture and accessories. Don't miss out on the best eggs Benedict and home-made cakes at **Manna Epicure**. Traffic up and down Kloof Street can be a nightmare during rush hours, so be prepared to wait a while, unless you're lucky on foot.

SEE ALSO FILM, P.52; RESTAURANTS, P.106

Kloof Nek Road ②

This is a relatively busy main road, running parallel to Kloof Street, that takes you in the direction of the Lower Cable Station (on Tafelberg Road)

Left: a cloudy day in the City Bowl.

Take afternoon high tea on the veranda of the **Mount Nelson Hotel** (accessible from Kloof Street), overlooking the manicured gardens, which has been host to royalty, A-list celebrities and international politicians for many years. The gourmet spread of sweet and savoury delights is worth every calorie after a hard day of shopping up a storm. *See also Hotels, p.63.*

and Signal Hill (at the top of the Nek) just before you head down into Camps Bay. Should you want to do the **Platteklip Gorge walk**, park your car at the cable station and zigzag your way up to the top of the mountain against steep rock face. It's about 3km (1¾ miles) and takes fit walkers about an hour to complete. Along Kloof Nek Road you'll find a selection of reasonable backpackers' lodges, internet cafés and bars. **Rafiki's** is a bohemian institution with a sweeping upstairs veranda overlooking Kloof Nek Road that comes alive in the early afternoon with sundowners (and is especially popular for its food specials). Heading up Kloof Nek on your right-hand side is the swish suburb of **Tamboerskloof** with its semi-detached Victorian townhouses, kiddies' play parks and funky corner cafés where locals meet.
SEE ALSO WALKS AND VIEWS, P.127

Suburbs

Upmarket residential suburbs range along the slopes of Table Mountain within the City Bowl. They include **Tamboerskloof**, **Higgovale**, **Oranjezicht** and **Gardens**. Here you'll find a great selection of boutique hotels, charming guesthouses and modern villas to rent with views overlooking the City centre and harbour. Most of these suburbs feature family-friendly parks on every corner, historic Cape Dutch homesteads (mostly occupied by diplomats and government ministers) and a variety of great neighbourhod restaurants, pizzerias and delis. In Gardens you can also visit South Africa's **Great Synagogue** and the **Jewish Museum** next door.
SEE ALSO CHURCHES, SYNAGOGUES AND MOSQUES, P.42; MUSEUMS AND GALLERIES, P.79

Left: the Platteklip Gorge walk; a distinctive house in Tamboerskloof.

Victoria and Alfred Waterfront and Robben Island

Better-known as the V&A Waterfront, this newly revitalised harbour of Cape has a range of uses, among them shopping, dining and a line-up of ever-changing entertainment and festivals that take place during the year. Just a short cruise away, you can visit Robben Island, the maximum security prison where Nelson Mandela spent 18 years of his 27-year imprisonment.

Victoria Wharf

One of the smartest shopping malls in the country, **Victoria Wharf** is a magnet for local and international tourists. If all you have is one day of shopping in Cape Town, then this is your best bet for getting that special something. At the east end of the shopping mall is the five-star **Table Bay** hotel.

SEE ALSO HOTELS, P.64; SHOPPING, P.119

Market Square ①

Linking Victoria Wharf with **Alfred Mall** (the quieter end of the V&A Waterfront, with a small selection of curio shops and cafés) you'll come across an open space better-known as the **Market Square**, which is a monthly venue for exhibitions and fairs. To one side of the square is the amphitheatre, a hot spot for concerts, festival events and street theatre over the warmer summer months. On most weekends you can catch live musical performances by local artists.

A great way to get an eyeful of the cultural microcosm of Cape Town is taking in some fresh, salty air on the Sea Point Promenade where you'll spot everything from Lycra-clad joggers, to speeding roller-bladers, lovers, stick-wielding oldies and dog walkers. It's an eye-opener like no other.

Clock Tower Precinct ②

Reach the **Clock Tower Precinct** via a swing bridge from Victoria Wharf – it swings aside to let boats pass into the marina. Built as the Port Captain's office in 1883, this Victorian tower with a distinctly Gothic look is a famous city landmark but also marks the original entrance to the docks. There are benches in the sun and a wide selection of cafés and places to eat around the tower and the **Clock Tower Centre**, which has a few luxury boutique shops for sunglasses and jewellery among other things. Here you'll also find the **Cape Town Tourism Office**, which is a good place to pick up information about

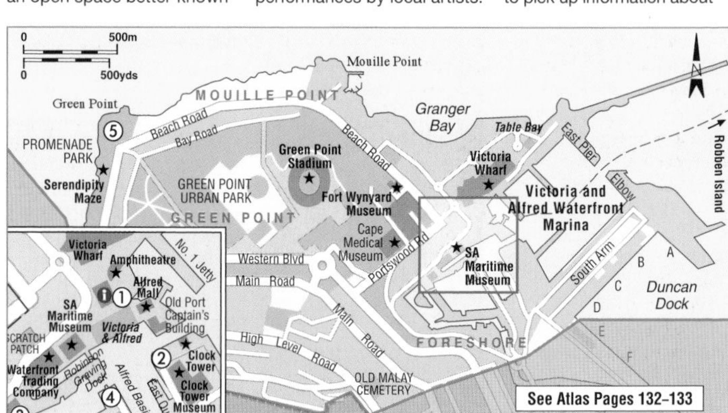

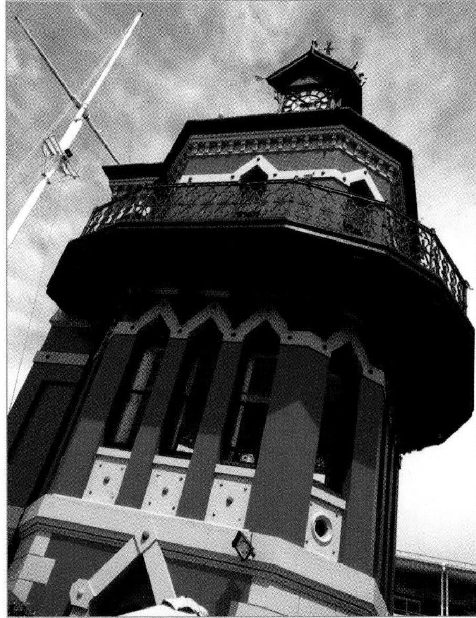

Left: the Clock Tower.

and other luxury developments, their sweeping sea views demanding sky-high real-estate prices. The **Green Point Lighthouse** ⑤, constructed in 1824 (now an official National Monument) still acts as a beacon for ships entering and leaving the harbour. You can't miss its bright red-and-white-striped façade, or the sound of the loud foghorn on misty nights. Visitors are welcome to climb up the spiraling stairs during weekdays for a quick tour.

Robben Island

See map, inside back cover. Jump on a ferry and visit this famous prison island, where Nelson Mandela was held captive for 18 years. The island has a remarkably varied history that goes back some 400 years. It's been a post office, a fishing base, a whaling station, a hospital, a mental asylum, a military base and, most infamously, 'South Africa's Alcatraz'. Lepers, slaves, the mentally ill, religious leaders, political activists and prisoners of war were all exiled here. Declared a World Heritage Site in 1999, visitors can now tour the island. There are no restaurants on the island.
SEE ALSO MUSEUMS AND GALLERIES, P.80

tours and activities in and around the city.
SEE ALSO ESSENTIALS, P.49

Two Oceans Aquarium ③

Just to the west of Victoria Wharf in Dock Road is the **Two Oceans Aquarium.** Probably the most exciting attraction at the Waterfront, this imaginatively designed three-level building contains more than 3,000 fish, mammals, birds, reptiles and plants. If you're in the mood for braving some icy-cold water, slip on a wetsuit and hop into the shark tank (with an experienced diver).
SEE ALSO CHILDREN, P.41

Chavonnes Battery ④

On the south side of the Waterfront under the BoE/Nedcor building are the 18th-century remains of **Chavonnes Battery**, a military installation built by the Dutch East India Company. Recently discovered when the nearby Clock Tower was under construction, it remained in use until the 19th century.

Green Point

The V&A Waterfront is a self-contained area, so most visitors don't venture around the shoreline to **Mouille Point** and **Green Point**, only a small stretch of which fronts the sea and is now lined with new upmarket apartment blocks

Right: Green Point Lighthouse and Robben Island.

Bo-Kaap

On the slopes of Signal Hill you'll find the suburb of Bo-Kaap. Home to a section of the Cape's Muslim community (often referred to as the Cape Malays), this is one of the city's oldest and most interesting areas, though its character is under threat by property developers looking to invest in this fascinating neighborhood. Also known as the Malay Quarter, its steep and narrow cobbled streets are squeezed tightly with brightly painted cottages, once the home to slaves, political prisoners and exiles. In 1950 under the Group Areas Act, the area was declared Muslim, and those who did not fit the profile were forced to leave.

Cape Malay Community

Bo-Kaap was originally a district of artisans brought in to assist with the development of a quickly growing town. As the town developed, the Europeans who lived here tended to move on to places like Woodstock and Mowbray, and the Muslim population moved in, particularly after 1834, when slaves were liberated.

The area is mostly associated with the Muslims who arrived in the Cape from 1658 onwards, as slaves, political exiles and convicts from East Africa and Southeast Asia. The political exiles tended to be people of high rank and culture, and from the beginning they bonded through their religion. They were known as Cape Malays – an incorrect term since the majority of Bo-Kaap's residents are of non-Malaysian descent. Many of today's residents are the descendants of skilled craftsmen, silversmiths, shoemakers, tailors, fishermen and cooks.

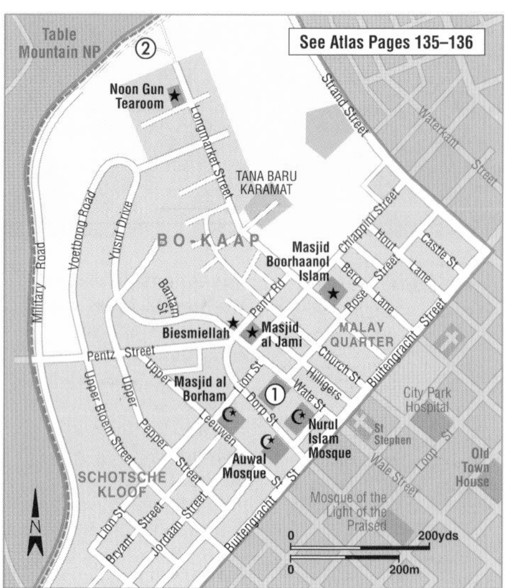

Architecture

Bo-Kaap was originally an area of *huurhuisies*, little houses for rent, put up by the landowner Jan de Waal on his property Walendorp in the 1780s. Today the streets are made up of rows of flat-roofed houses, each with two rooms at the front facing the street and a narrow passage up the middle. Many have little roofless stoeps in front of them, and a courtyard at the back in which inhabitants can cool off in summer. Originally

Left: Bo-Kaap with Signal Hill in the backround.

New Year celebrations in the Bo-Kaap come alive with a throng of banjo-playing minstrels dressed in flamboyant suits dancing through the streets in commemoration of the Tweede Nuwe Jaar (Second New Year). The festival was traditionally confined to 2 January, the only day in the calendar when slaves were allowed to down their tools and enjoy a holiday.

Bo-Kaap Ramble

Grassroutes Tours will pick you up from your hotel and drop you off at the Bo-Kaap Museum. Visit the Auwal Mosque *(see p.42)*, the Kramats (Muslim shrines), and nibble on some traditional Cape Malay food. For more details tel: 021 422 1671.

roofs were made of a mixture of whale oil and molasses, and were hidden behind a curved parapet. Many homes have their original sash windows – and original glazing.

Bo-Kaap proper, and the adjacent streets, make up Cape Town's largest concentration of architecture predating 1850. Some are still lived in by descendants of the original owners. Many have been restored and are painted in bright colours. To learn more about the area, visit the small but illuminating **Bo-Kaap Museum** ① on Wale Street. One block south, at Dorp Street, is **Auwal**, South Africa's oldest mosque, dating back to 1795 and said to be where Afrikaans was first taught.

SEE ALSO CHURCHES, SYNAGOGUES AND MOSQUES, P.42; MUSEUMS AND GALLERIES, P.77

Noon Gun ②

A fitting end to a tour of Bo-Kaap would be a meal at **Biesmiellah** or the **Noon Gun Tearoom**, set in a Bo-Kaap home on Longmarket Street. Situated on Signal Hill, the Noon Gun has been operational since 1806 and is named for the cannon fired by the South African Navy daily at noon that has informed Capetonians of their lunch break ever since. The noon gun has been fired automatically since 1864 by a signal it receives from South Africa's master clock at the South African Astronomical Observatory in Sutherland – they are the oldest guns in daily use in the world. Enjoy a traditional *melktert* (milk tart) at the Noon Gun Tearoom and Restaurant with its magnificent views of the city and mountain.

SEE ALSO RESTAURANTS, P.108

Left and right: Bo-Kaap's colourful architecture.

Southern Suburbs

Follow the M3 out of the city on De Waal Drive around the base of Devil's Peak and you will arrive in the leafy Southern Suburbs of Cape Town. This is the collective name for a string of old villages that grew up as the road to Muizenberg developed and after the railway line to Simon's Town opened in the 1860s. Predominantly a residential area, you'll notice the lush green landscape, especially when you venture along the upper fringes of Newlands Forest and Bishopscourt, where Kirstenbosch links up with Constantia. There are some exceptional monuments and several grand estates from the colonial era in this area.

Observatory

Observatory derives its name from the Royal Observatory established in 1821, and is a popular and very bohemian old neighbourhood. Commonly known as Obz, it's filled with bars, cafés and cheap-and-cheerful restaurants that usually stay open until the early hours of the morning. The architecture is mostly Victorian terrace houses with ornate 'broekie lace' decorations and cast-iron balconies. It's also home to South Africa's famous **Groote Schuur Hospital**, where the world's first heart transplant was performed in 1967.

Rosebank

This quiet neighbourhood is considered the academic hub of Cape Town due to its proximity to the University of Cape Town. Beautiful Victorian homes and Edwardian villas flanked by large palm trees characterise this area. Highlights include **Mostert's Mill**, a working windmill dating back to 1796 that has been restored, complete with a thatch cap that rotates to catch the wind. Just below is the **Irma Stern Museum**, which was once the home of the great South African painter Irma Stern, who lived here for 40 years.

SEE ALSO MUSEUMS AND GALLERIES, P.81

> Newlands was chosen as the site of Cape Town's breweries because of the freshness of the mountain water. An old malthouse and the old Ohlsson brewery have been restored, and visitors can take a tour to understand just how special South African beer really is.

Rhodes Memorial ①

Just next to the University of Cape Town campus is the **Rhodes Memorial**, Herbert Baker's classical monument to Cecil John Rhodes, who donated all the land along the lower slope of the mountain to the city of Cape Town. Built in 1905, the impressive U-shaped building with Doric columns and a massive flight of steps provides great views across to northern Cape Town, the Cape Flats and the Hottentots Holland mountain range to the east. It's a lovely place to walk or have a picnic – just avoid coming here after dark as it is very isolated.

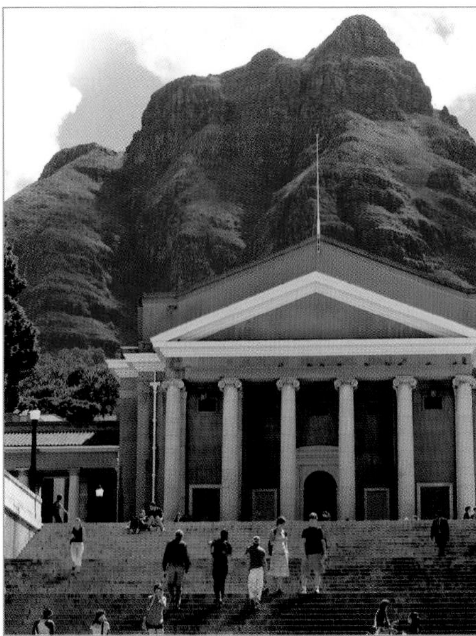

Left: the beautifully situated University of Cape Town.

University of Cape Town ②

Built on the former Groote Schuur Estate land, the University of Cape Town is worth taking a stroll around. Founded in 1829, this was the first university in the country, and today its architecture and medical faculties are world-renowned, attracting national and international students.
SEE ALSO ARCHITECTURE, P.28

Rondebosch

Rondebsoch grew up around a garden established by the early Dutch colonists. In the late 19th century it was one of the smartest areas and popular with the English, who were keen to demonstrate their status. Rondebosch is also famous for its schools.

Newlands

In the early 1700s Willem Adriaan van der Stel created a new garden for the colony and established oak plantations in the vicinity which you can see along Newlands Avenue. Newlands is also associated with cricket and rugby. On Campground Road is the famous **Sahara Park** cricket ground. On Boundary Road is the equally renowned **Newlands Rugby Stadium** ③, the second-oldest test stadium in the world. Nearby is the South African Newlands Breweries, oen of the world's largest.
SEE ALSO SPORT, P.120

Claremont ④

Beyond Newlands is Claremont, one of the commercial hubs of the Southern Suburbs. Newly renovated **Cavendish Square** is a huge shopping mall with a top-end range of fashion boutiques, smart interior studios, bookshops, two cinema complexes and good restaurants.
SEE ALSO SHOPPING, P.119

Wynberg

Continuing southwest along the M3 highway you'll come to Wynberg. It grew up as a garrison village around a late-18th-century military camp. Today its charming, narrow streets are lined with Regency-style cottages, many of them interior-design shops, art galleries and a handful of restaurants.

Tokai Forest

More pine plantation than forest, this is a good spot to enjoy a picnic or a brisk walk. The forest's historic arboretum houses over 247 tree species from all over the globe, and about 15 fungus species also sprout here, some of which are edible. There is also a small café where you can tuck into a healthy breakfast or home-cooked lunch.
SEE ALSO WALKS AND VIEWS, P.128

Right: Claremont locals.

Constantia Valley and Kirstenbosch

Constantia Valley is one of the country's most important national treasures; it's also home to the city's most exclusive addresses, with the lush surrounds of the Cape's oldest wine-producing areas attracting the rich and famous looking for some privacy. The cultural landscape here derives from the earliest days of the colony, when the original land grants were handed out and farms were established to supply vegetables and fruit to the Dutch East India Company.

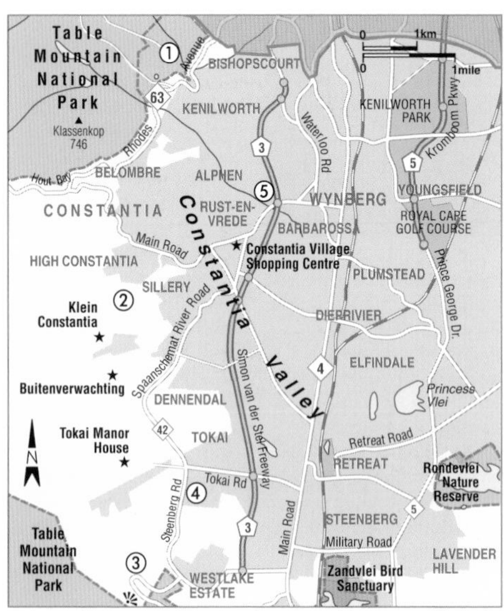

Kirstenbosch National Botanical Gardens ①

Situated on the eastern slopes of Table Mountain, this 528-hectare (1,320-acre) estate and green lung of the city is possibly one of the most beautiful gardens in the world. With its shaded lawns and gurgling streams it's also blanketed in a diverse range of fynbos (a scrubland indigenous to the Western Cape) and other native flora and fauna. Impressive features include a sculpture garden, an enormous conservatory, deserts and shaded forests, a braille trail, and a fragrance garden where you can pick flowers and rub them between your fingers to extract their unique smells and in some instances their powerful medicinal values. There are various restaurants and tearooms on the premises and some excellent, secluded picnic spots. Their annual summer sunset concerts are a must.

SEE ALSO MUSIC, DANCE AND THEATRE, P.87; PARKS AND RESERVES, P.97; WALKS AND VIEWS, P.128

Groot Constantia ②

The Constantia Valley is also the cradle of the South African Wine Industry. Vines were first planted here in the 17th century by Cape Governor Simon van der Stel, who founded **Groot Constantia**, the magnificent Cape Dutch home he occupied from 1699–1712. Besides drinking wine, guests can dine out on gourmet food at their two acclaimed restaurants, including **Jonkershuis**, or picnic under the trees. Visitors can also visit an exhibition of the estate's history, including the historic Cloete cellar, now housing a wine museum. The manor house itself is also open to the pub-

Constantia's famous dessert wine, Vin de Constance, so treasured by great names of 18th-century Europe, is today made in much the same way by Klein Constantia (part of the Constantia Estate until 1712). Visit Klein Constantia to sample this nectar – you can only purchase it on the estate.

Left: the vineyards at Groot Constantia.

lic and houses an esteemed collection of period furniture.
SEE ALSO FOOD AND DRINK, P.57; RESTAURANTS, P.109

Steenberg ③

Steenberg (meaning mountain of stone) is the oldest wine farm in the Cape, lying just below Steenberg Mountain. Ten years after Jan van Riebeeck arrived on these shores, Catherina Ustings Ras, a formidable settler, asked Simon van der Stel for a piece of land. It was here that her Cape Dutch Manor house was erected in 1695, the same year the very first wine was produced. Today her estate's wines are reaping in many local and international accolades, and its restaurant, **Catharina's**, is a gourmet hot spot. For those who want to make a weekend of it, the estate has its own five-star hotel housed in the original 17th-century buildings, now declared a national monument. Go for a comprehensive wine-tasting and wine tour, the Sauvignon Blanc is particularly noteworthy.
SEE ALSO FOOD AND DRINK, P.57; HOTELS, P.65; RESTAURANTS, P.108

Pollsmoor Prison ④

Steenberg estate is directly opposite Pollsmoor Prison, where Nelson Mandela was moved from Robben Island in 1982. His conditions in Pollsmoor Prison were considerably better than at Robben Island, and his move here represented a turning point in relations between the government and the ANC.

Alphen Estate ⑤

Not far away and quite different from Steenberg, Alphen is one of the finest houses in the Cape. Its estate came into existence in 1712 following the death of Simon van der Stel, who at one point owned all the land from Groot Constantia to Wynberg Hill. Built in the middle of the 18th century, the architecture of Alphen is quite different from any other building of this period. Rather than the more usual Cape Dutch gable, it's a two-storey property with massive pediments front and back. Alphen passed through many owners, ending up in the possession of the Cloete family (who also owned Groot Constantia). Today it is a hotel and filled with wonderful furniture pieces and collectables.

Right: Kirstenbosch National Botanical Gardens.

Atlantic Seaboard, Cape Peninsula and Table Mountain National Park

The sweep of shore extending from the V&A Waterfront to Cape Point offers some sensational 'Cape Riviera' coastline, a mix of prime real estate and pristine beaches bordering the chilly Atlantic Ocean. On the other hand, the Cape Peninsula is one of South Africa's great natural landscapes with its brilliant sequence of mountains along the way.

Table Mountain National Park ①

Table Mountain and its accompaniments, Devil's Peak, Lion's Head and Signal Hill, were known as *Hoerikwaggo* (Mountains in the Sea) to the early indigenous Khoikhoi. However, these famous landmarks form only part of the Table Mountain National Park, which since 1998 has been massively extended to include about 73 percent of the entire Cape Peninsula. Take in the breath-taking views across False Bay and the Cape Flats to the Hottentots Holland Mountains in the east and to Blouberg and the beginning of the west coast in the north. **Maclear's Beacon** is its highest point.

SEE ALSO PARKS AND RESERVES, P.96; WALKS AND VIEWS, P.126

Lion's Head and Signal Hill

This jutting peak derives its unusual name from its profile resembling the head of a lion. A little further down is **Signal Hill**, making up the rump. A must-do is a sunset or early-morning walk up **Lion's Head**. Be sure to wear sturdy walking shoes as it takes about 45 minutes and there are tricky bits near the summit. Once at the top you will be rewarded with mind-blowing views over the City Bowl and Atlantic Seaboard. Being a popular tourist spot, it has increasingly become a target spot for muggings so don't come here alone or at night.

SEE ALSO WALKS AND VIEWS, 127

The Cableway

The cableway opened in 1929 and by the end of the 20th century had carried some 13.5 million people up to the summit. Today there are new cars capable of carrying 64 passengers that rotate 360 for the best views of the rock face, the city and coastline.

Sea Point

Situated between the seaward side of the rump of Lion's Head and the coastline of Table Bay, just before it merges with the Atlantic Ocean is Sea Point – a busy, noisy and slightly seedy part of town littered with garish 1970s high-rise apartments, dodgy nightclubs and porn shops. Recently the neighbourhood has seen a considerable upgrade, with property suddenly shooting up in value.

SEE ALSO BEACHES, P.39

The cableway is completely dependent on the weather, and if you are in Cape Town out of season you are advised to make your trip to Table Mountain on the first clear day of your stay in case you don't get another chance. Even on a clear day the cableway doesn't operate if it is very windy. It's best to call before you head out.

Left: Camps Bay.

Bantry Bay and Clifton

Hugging the steep mountainside beneath Lion's Head, **Bantry Bay** is a lovely small seaside neighbourhood characterised by Victorian villas with palms and bougainvillea, reminiscent of coastal towns along the French Riviera. Its neighbour **Clifton** has four wind-free coves, each one an amphitheatre lined with beach bungalows and otherwise known as 'millionaires' playground'.

SEE ALSO BEACHES, P.37

Camps Bay ②

Catch a glimpse of the Twelve Apostles as you wind down into Camps Bay. Often very windy, this expensive suburb with its palm-lined beach is jam-packed with trendy sidewalk cafés, bars and restaurants, which range from simple to swanky.

SEE ALSO BEACHES, P.36

Hout Bay

Hout Bay is a busy little harbour with many informal spots to buy fish and chips. Take a trip out to Duiker Island to see the 7,000-strong colony of Cape fur seals. There's not much left of the village's old character, although there is a pretty stone-built Anglican church of St Peter the Fisherman dating from 1895.

Kalk Bay

A pretty seaside village that acquired its name from the lime kilns located here in the early days of the colony. Capetonians come here to trawl antique and bric-a-brac shops or art galleries then grab a bite to eat at one of many casual delis, like the **Olympia Café and Deli** for the best brunch in town. There are some great beaches close by at **St James**.

SEE ALSO BEACHES, P.39; RESTAURANTS, P.111

Simon's Town ③

The headquarters of the South African Navy, Simon's Town has one of the densest clusters of old buildings in the country, and many of them are still used. The town also has excellent restaurants, antique shops and galleries. Visit the penguins at **Boulders Beach**.

SEE ALSO BEACHES, P.36

Cape Point

The **Cape of Good Hope Nature Reserve** is most famous for Cape Point, the furthest tip of the Cape Peninsula. There are a number of drives and picnic sites which are home to baboons, zebra, eland, red hartebeest, ostrich and pretty bontebok. Take the funicular to the viewing platforms where you can watch the lashing ocean.

SEE ALSO PARKS AND RESERVES, P.97; WALKS AND VIEWS, P.129

Right: the cableway's views.

Cape Winelands

South Africa has 13 designated wine routes, of which the area called the Winelands – comprising the routes of Helderberg (Somerset West), Stellenbosch, Paarl and Franschhoek – is by far the most popular. Plan a day trip or get away for a quiet weekend and take in the breathtaking mountains, rolling vineyards, historic estates and, most importantly, some star-rated fruits of the vine. Many old vineyards have since been made into hotels and restaurants, or have incorporated them into their estates. Although not cheap, they do offer the chance to stay a night, or enjoy a meal in wonderful surroundings.

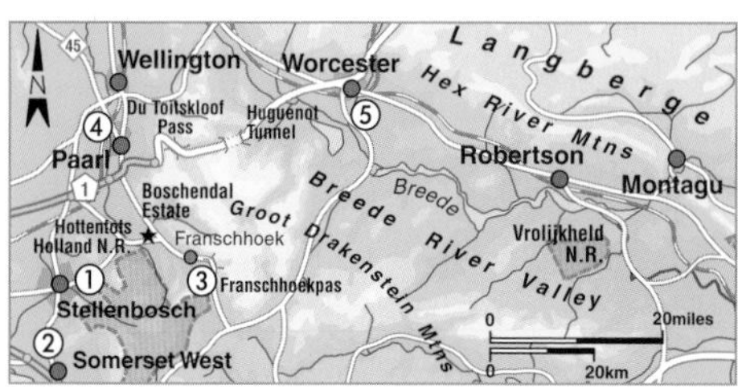

Stellenbosch ①

Less than an hour away from the Mother City, the second-oldest town in South Africa, **Stellenbosch** is 27 years Cape Town's junior, founded in 1679. Today it's the site of the country's premier Afrikaans university, as well as the epicentre of the burgeoning Cape wine industry.

Start exploring on Dorp (village) Street, which runs parallel to the Eersterivier (First River), lined by the longest row of pre-20th-century buildings anywhere in South Africa. These include the quaint Oom Samie's se Winkel (Uncle Samie's Shop) and a Lutheran church of 1851. The significant student population of this small town ensures a lively night out on the town, whether it's a pint of beer in a rowdy pub or a swish wine lounge. The town is studded with fine-dining restaurants serving French-style cuisine and local Cape Malay Fare.

SEE ALSO FOOD AND DRINK, P.57

Somerset West ②

About 20km (12 miles) south of Stellenbosch and 40km (24 miles) southeast of Cape Town you'll arrive in Somerset West and the famous **Helderberg Wine Route**. A highlight is the **Vergelegen** wine estate, which translates as 'Far Away', founded in 1700 by William van der Stel (son of Simon). The **Cape Dutch manor house**, now a private museum, is decorated in period style and set in a garden surrounded by enormous camphor trees. For something active, you may want to take a walk or stroll through the **Helderberg Nature Reserve,** recognised for the endemic disa orchid, an exquisite red flower that blooms between January and March.

SEE ALSO WALKS AND VIEWS, P.129

Franschhoek ③

Taking a drive out into Franschhoek is probably one of the more scenic trips as it skirts

Left: approaching Somerset West.

Left: Stellenbosch.

> Nelson Mandela spent the last two years of his imprisonment (1988–90) in Victor Verster Prison, near Paarl. Unlike the harsh conditions of Robben Island, Victor Verster was a comfortable and spacious villa.

the northern slope of the **Groot Drakenstein Mountains** via the **Helshoogte** (Hell's Heights) **Pass** into the sprawling village of **Franschhoek**, meaning French Corner, only 28km (17 miles) from Stellenbosch, and encircled by craggy mountain peaks (usually snow-capped in the winter). This is where the Huguenots who left France in the early 18th century settled. Today there is a tangible French influence in both the food (*see p.112–13* for some of the country's best restaurants) and in the wine industry. You can see this influence in the names of the estates, which include **Chamonix**, **Dieu Donné** and **Mont Rochelle** among others. Visit the 300-year-old **Boschendal Estate** with its attractive Cape Dutch manor house lined by an avenue of ancient trees. This is a popular picnic spot in the summer months.

SEE ALSO FOOD AND DRINK, P.57; WALKS AND VIEWS, P.129

Paarl ④

Founded on the banks of the Berg River in 1720, **Paarl** was given to the Huguenot settlers in 1687. A short 45-minute drive from Cape Town along the N1 highway, the town centre is rather dreary in comparison with its neighbouring Boland towns in terms of architecture, although an acclaimed wine route offers access to some of the country's most revered wine estates and fine dining establishments. The **Afrikaans Language Museum** celebrate the Afrikaans language. Adjacent to the town is the **Paarl Mountain Nature Reserve**, the slopes of which hold the **Afrikaans Taal Monument**.

SEE ALSO FOOD AND DRINK, P.57; LANGUAGE, P.70; PARKS AND RESERVES, P.98

Worcester ⑤

A little further afield is the attractive Boland town of **Worcester**, which lies in the Breede River Valley at the base of the **Hex River Mountains**. The mountains rise to 2,250 metres (7,382ft) and form the highest peaks in the Western Cape. Founded in 1820 and named after the Marquis of Worcester, the elder brother of then Governor of the Cape, Lord Charles Somerset, the town is noted for its elegant **Drostdy**, regarded as the country's finest example of Cape Regency architecture. There's also a neo-Gothic Dutch reformed **Moederkerk** built in 1824.

Right: The Taal Monument in Paarl. *Taal* means language.

Overberg

During the 17th century, the Dutch settlers saw the jagged Hottentots Holland mountain range as the Cape Colony's natural border, beyond which lay what they called Overberg, meaning 'over the mountain'. Today this coastal area wedged between the Cape Peninsula and the Garden Route, with mountains lining its northern border and the ocean on the south, varies from fruit orchards to grain fields to fynbos-covered hills, and parks and reserves to explore. A clutch of pretty resort towns along the coast provide opportunities to meet some of the Cape's unique wildlife, including whales off Hermanus and African penguins at Betty's Bay.

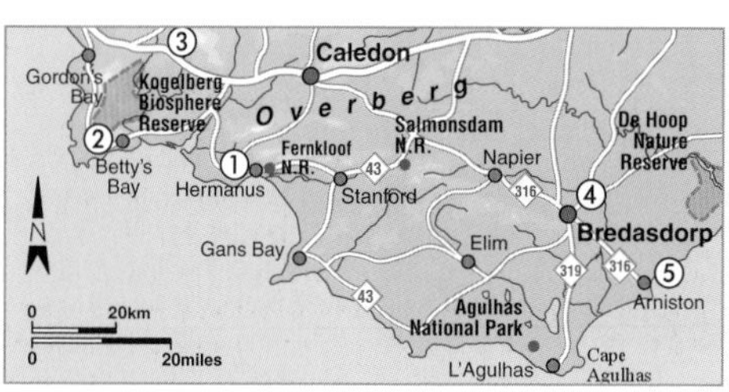

South Africa's national bird is the elegant and beautiful **Blue crane**. The Blue crane is the smallest of the crane species and found mainly in the Overberg and Swartland regions of the Western Cape, which is home to a population of approximately 20,000 individuals. The Blue crane's natural habitat within this region is dry grasslands and shallow wetlands, but it has adapted well to the artificial grasslands created by the farming systems in the Overberg region.

Hermanus ①

A main focus for tourism in the Overberg region, this small seaside town was founded in 1857 by German settlers who named it Hermanuspietersfontein (Hermanus Pieter's Spring) in remembrance of a shepherd who used the site as his regular summer encampment. Today it's a resort town for a wealthy elite of holiday-home owners who meet here over the summer season. The town itself with its cobbled alleys and café society retains the quaint feel of an old-world fishing village. Its main claim to fame is that it's the world's top site for land-based whale viewing. Every year between June and November over 100 Southern right whales congregate for the mating and calving season. Watch them breach and lobtail in the water just 30 metres (100ft) below vantage points like Castle Rock overlooking the Old Harbour.

Left: the resort town of Hermanus.

Betty's Bay ②

This pretty resort town on the R44 back towards Cape Town is also known for its colony of African penguins at Stony Point and the waterfall-strewn fynbos of the **Harold Porter National Botanical Gardens** below the Kogelberg Mountains. For dedicated hikers and botanists the vast **Kogelberg Biosphere Reserve** protects the most diverse montane fynbos habitat in the Cape with more than 1,500 plant species identified. The reserve lies 6km (4 miles) from Kleinmond on the R44 between Hermanus and Betty's Bay. Four hiking trails run through the reserve, and there's canoeing on the Palmiet River.
SEE ALSO PARKS AND RESERVES, P.99–100

Elgin and Grabouw ③

Leaving Cape Town you will ascend Sir Lowry's Pass to

Left: African penguins at Betty's Bay.

reach the fruit-growing areas of **Grabouw** and **Elgin**. The area produces 65 percent of South Africa's apple export crop and has many farm stalls selling the best local farm produce and traditional treats. The Overberg's wine estates form a triangle between Grabouw, Villiersdorp and passing through the Bot River to the southernmost vineyards in the Hemel-en-Aarde Valley near Hermanus. Only until recently have Grabouw and Elgin started to produce some award-winning wines, including Iona Vineyards' Sauvignon Blanc and Ross Gower's Pinot Noir Brut.

Cape Agulhas

Situated in the Eastern Overberg almost 200km (120 miles) from the Cape of Good Hope, Cape Agulhas is the official meeting point of the Indian and Atlantic oceans and the most southerly point on the African continent. Rather underwhelming in comparison with Cape Point, Agulhas, which was coined by early Portuguese navigators and translates as 'needles', is characterised by the jagged rocks that lie offshore and that accounted for at least 250 shipwrecks.

Bredasdorp and Arniston

Bredasdorp ④ is one of those unassuming back-road towns that's slowly becoming more popular as a weekend getaway. It has several antique and gift shops, a thriving handmade candle factory called Kapula, and a handful of simple country restaurants for good farm food. It's also en route to Agulhus and noted for its **Shipwreck Museum** with treasures from ships wrecked off the Agulhus coast.

Just as rewarding is a detour from Bredasdorp to **Arniston** ⑤, named in memory of a ship that ran aground there in 1852 claiming 352 lives. The fishing village with its 19th-century whitewashed thatched fishermen's cottages has been declared a National Monument. It's often referred to by its pre-1852 name Waenhuiskrans (Wagon House Cliff), which refers to a nearby cavern large enough to house several ox-wagons, accessible only at low tide. Running for some 50km (30 miles) along the coast east of Arniston is the **De Hoop Nature Reserve**, protecting the largest coastal fynbos habitat. SEE ALSO PARKS AND RESERVES, P.99

Right: the spectacular Overberg farmlands.

Garden Route

The Garden Route is one of the country's most popular tourist destinations after Cape Town, drawing visitors to its wild forests, unspoilt beaches, freshwater lakes, hidden valleys and imposing mountains towards the forested shores of the Tsitsikamma National Park. This is a distinctly African garden – no European-style manicured lawns with neat formal layouts. Its timeless appeal both to foreign travellers and to South African holidaymakers is reflected in a booming guesthouse and hotel industry, not to mention the region's ever-escalating property prices. Time allowing, the best way to reach the Garden Route is via the Klein Karoo.

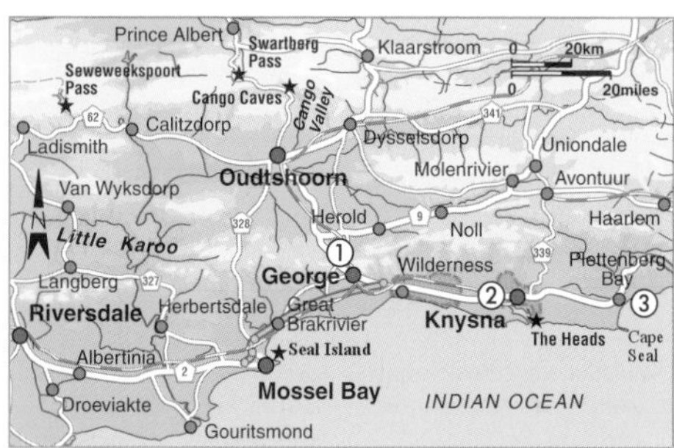

Mossel Bay

Regarded as the beginning of the Garden Route, **Mossel Bay** is where Portuguese navigator Bartolomew Diaz dropped anchor in 1488, becoming the first European on South African soil. The **Bartolomew Diaz Museum Complex** is dedicated to his memory and includes exhibitions of shells and shipping. The town is still a popular holiday resort, with its many beaches and safe rock pools. It has also become a growing industrial centre since the discovery of oil and natural gas off the coast.

George ①

Leaving Mossel Bay on the N2, head towards the lumber village of **George**, founded in 1811 at the base of the Outeniqua Mountains. A pretty inland town, George is anything but small, with a population of over 150,000. It offers a good range of tourist facilities and is a good base for day trips along the Garden Route and the Little Karoo. Spot several fine buildings, including the Dutch Reformed **Moederkerk** and the elegant **Public Library**. Outside the library is the **Slave Tree**, a broad oak tree where the slave market once took place. The **George Museum** in Courtenay Street has an exhibition devoted to the years of Apartheid under the rule of President P.W. Botha.

Oudtshoorn

Located roughly 60km (36 miles) north of George, **Oudtshoorn** is a popular day trip off the Garden Route and the main town of the **Little Karoo**, an arid region which derives its name from a Khoi word for dry. Once a celebrated ostrich-feather centre, Jewish traders from Eastern Europe came here to set up ostrich farms and made fortunes exporting the feathers to

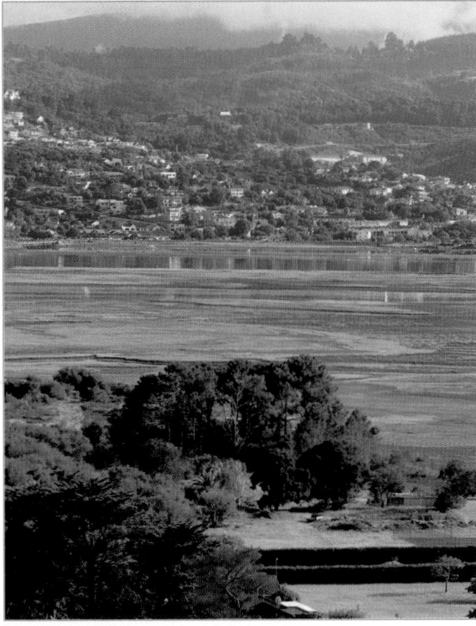

Left: Knysna and the Knysna lagoon.

Take a relatively inexpensive boat excursion to nearby Seal Island, where hundreds of Cape fur seals can be seen basking on the rocks. For adrenalin-junkies there are also caged shark dives arranged by local operators to view predatory Great whites in action.

Europe. The **C.P. Nel Museum** has displays on the history of the ostrich boom. Today the ostrich industry still thrives, although the skins are now more sought after in the fashion world. There are several farms open to the public. Another highlight 32km (20 miles) north of Oudtshoorn are the **Cango Caves**, which extend into the Swartberg Mountains.

Swartberg Pass

Past the caves, the R328 takes you towards the up-and-coming village of **Prince Albert**, with its Victorian homes and whitewashed cottages. To get there you will have to wind through one of the most beautiful mountain passes in South Africa, the 1,436-metre (4,700ft) **Swartberg Pass**. Built between 1881 and 1888 and now a National Monument, the views are magnificent, but not for those who suffer from vertigo.

Left: ostriches at Little Karoo.

Seweweekspoort Pass

If the Swartberg Pass is not challenging enough for the overland explorer, take an alternative route via the **Seweweekspoort Pass** across the mountains. First opened in 1857, this pass crosses the River Groot over 30 times along its 17km (11-mile) length, snaking through bare walls of vertical rock. Red sandstone and milky quartz hang above you on the road. Check the weather before you take this route as it's usually closed after heavy rains.

Knysna ②

From George, still heading straight on the N2, bypass **Wilderness**, a bustling little resort town with a long stretch of sandy beaches, towards the busier town of **Knysna**. It was founded at the beginning of the 19th century by George Rex (rumoured to be an illegitimate son of King George III). Pretty seaside cottages and larger waterfront mansions on the Knysna lagoon make this a popular holiday spot throughout the year. The mouth of the canal is flanked by two huge sandstone cliffs known as **The Heads**. Enjoy oysters and an icy glass of wine at the private **Featherbed Nature Reserve** overlooking the lagoon. A good place for arts and crafts is **Thesen House**. Don't leave without sampling a glass of beer from **Mitchell's Brewery** on Arend Street.

SEE ALSO PARKS AND RESERVES, P.100

Plettenberg Bay ③

Next stop is South Africa's most luxurious seaside resort, 32km (20 miles) east of Knysna with its golden stretch of beaches, warm sea water and massive seafront holiday homes. Fondly known as 'Plett', some of the country's wealthiest individuals descend on this coastal town over the festive season. **Robberg Nature Reserve**, the rocky peninsula on the western side of the bay, offers excellent vantage points for whale-watching. Snorkelling, diving, fishing and tree-swinging are just a few other activities to keep you busy.

SEE ALSO PARKS AND RESERVES, P.100

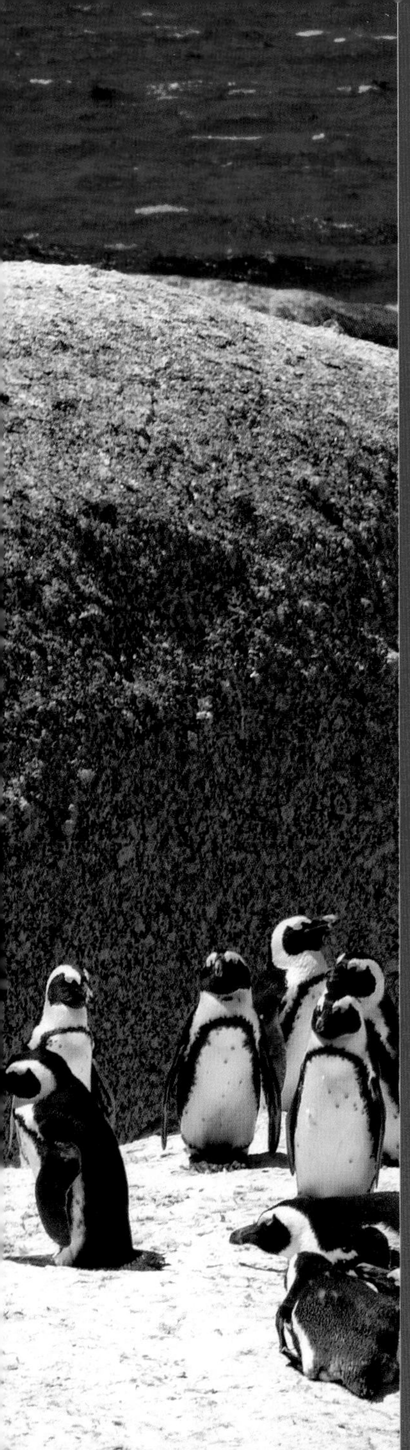

A–Z

In the following section Cape Town's attractions and services are organised by theme, under alphabetical headings. Items that link to another theme are cross-referenced. All sights that fall within the atlas section at the end of the book are given a page number and grid reference.

Architecture

Architecture aficionados coming to Cape Town for the first time will discover a wealth of building vernaculars: the beautiful buildings of the Cape Dutch period (17th and 18th centuries); the work of internationally acclaimed architect Sir Herbert Baker; preserved Art Deco buildings favoured by architects in the 1930s; and an impressive variety of newly built modern-contemporary homes on the Atlantic Seaboard and in the Southern Suburbs. Spend a day walking the streets appreciating some of the new (and surviving) structures that form part of a colourful city skyline.

Left: the Castle of Good Hope.

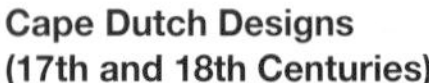

Cape Dutch Designs (17th and 18th Centuries)

Castle of Good Hope
Corner of Buitenkant and Darling streets, City Centre; tel: 021 787 1249; www.castleofgoodhope.co.za; daily 9am–4pm; entrance charge; map p.136 B3
The oldest reminder of the role that the Dutch played in the city's history remains a fascinating place to explore. Today's pentagonal fortification replaced a small clay-and-timber fort built in 1652 by Commander Jan van Riebeeck, founder of the maritime replenishment station at the Cape of Good Hope. In 1664 there were renewed rumours of war between Britain and the Netherlands, and a British attack on the Cape was feared. During that same year Commander Zacharius Wagenaer was instructed to build a five-pointed stone castle built of brick (imported from Holland) and stone, with lime from Robben Island and is typical of Dutch colonial settlements from America to Asia. The bell at the entrance was cast in Amsterdam in 1697 and looks much as it has for centuries.
SEE ALSO MUSEUMS AND GALLERIES, P.76

Before the British arrived with their Georgian and Victorian architectural styles, the Dutch stamped their own style on many buildings that remain today. The so-called **Cape Dutch style** is characteristically gabled, low and whitewashed, usually shaped by the materials most readily at hand and the limited availability of well-trained craftsman.

Sir Herbert Baker (19th and 20th Centuries)

Groote Schuur Estate
Klipper Road, Rondebosch, Southern Suburbs; tel: 021 686 9100; tours by arrangement; entrance charge
Groote Schuur (Dutch for 'Big Barn') was originally built by the Dutch East India Company in about 1657 as part of the company's granary. In 1893 Cecil John Rhodes invited Sir Herbert Baker to remodel his Cape mansion in the Cape style and tradition combined with Arts and Crafts influences. The buildings have recently been restored, housing a private collection of books, Batavian and Cape Dutch furniture, porcelain, paintings and tapestries which belonged to Rhodes.

University of Cape Town
Slopes of Devil's Peak, Rondebosch, Southern Suburbs; tel: 021 650 3121;

Right: ornate coping; University of Cape Town.

Left: the Castle of Good Hope.

www.uct.ac.za; tours by arrangement; free
Built on land donated by Rhodes, you can't miss the series of imposing creeper-clad buildings with brick-red roof tiles on the M3 highway that straddle the eastern foothills of Devil's Peak. As the oldest university in the country, it's known for its sustained opposition to Apartheid during the struggle years. Take a breather on the Jamie Steps overlooking Table Bay or take a short drive to Hiddingh Campus (home of the drama and fine-art faculties) in the City Centre, which houses three theatres and an art gallery.

There are plenty of **Art Deco**: houses and apartment blocks in Sea Point, Vredehoek and more commercial buildings in the City Centre. Most of them are restored, and some of the prime examples in Sea Point are spacious sea-facing apartments looking out towards Robben Island.

Art Deco (1930s)

Art Deco marked a distinctive break in the way South Africans viewed themselves. No longer looking towards Britain and the colonial way (Victorian and neoclassical styles), construction boomed after the Great Depression with many landmark Art Deco buildings. However, most of them were torn down in the 1980s, while others fell into disrepair.

In recent years, Art Deco architectural devotees have revived some remaining buildings, namely **Mutual Heights**, previously the Old Mutual banking building in Darling Street. Step inside an enormous marble banking hall with a stone frieze depicting the history of South Africa. Today it is the reception for an upmarket apartment block. On Parliament Street there are massive stone figures representing African tribesman also in Deco style. A map plotting Cape Town's Art Deco buildings is available from the Tourism Visitors Centre in Burg Street.

Contemporary

A new wave of modern domestic architecture includes the slick seaside villas on the Atlantic Seaboard by Stefan Antoni, and the work of Van der Merwe Miszewski, who make the most of the city's views and indigenous landscape. Considering the easy, laid-back lifestyle in Cape Town, there is a strong focus on outdoor living, changing light, topography and the surrounding architecture.

Bars

Cape Town's bars are largely relaxed, informal watering holes frequented by loyal crowds. But that doesn't mean the city lacks an edge, aesthetic sensibility or any number of cosmopolitan destinations worth a visit. From the quirky bars lining the entertainment hub of Long Street in the city to the pink-friendly clubs of Green Point and the beach bars along the Atlantic Seaboard of Camps Bay, Cape Town has a bit of everything. Choose from English-style pubs, wine bars, live-music venues, gastro pubs, sundowner spots and late-night clubs. *See also Gay and Lesbian, p.58; Music, Dance and Theatre, p.86–7; Nightlife, p.90–3.*

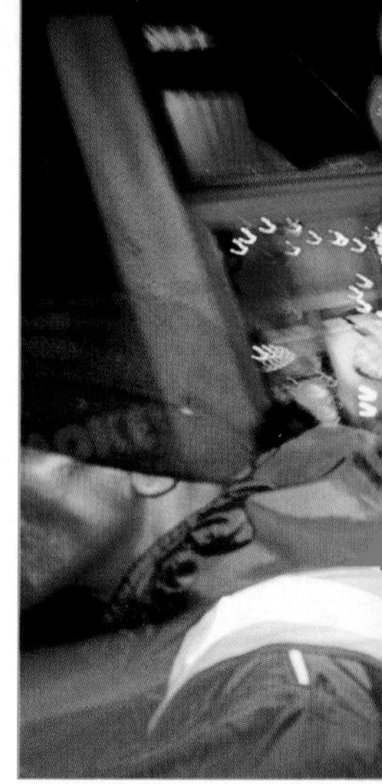

City Centre

The Dubliner

251 Long Street; tel: 021 424 1212; www.thedubliner.co.za; daily 10.30am–2am; map p.136 A2

Downstairs, the formerly staid Dubliner has become increasingly popular at weekends with a young tourist set enjoying the good-natured cocktail of loud music, dancing and booze that Irish pubs like this always seems to get right. Upstairs The Dubliner Lounge has an older vibe with live jazz, leather chairs and a wide choice of whiskies and cigars.

Fireman's Arms

Corner of Buitengracht and Mechau streets; tel: 021 419 1513; Mon–Sat 11am–12pm; map p.136 B1

Cape Town is not old in the European sense, but there are a few establishments that have been going for a fairly long time. This 'olde' English pub, established in 1864, is one of the stalwarts. Having fought off developers for years, The Fireman's Arms manages to retain its charm despite being surrounded by modern blocks. It features solid pub fare, fiery pizzas, big-screen TVs for sport, and a pub quiz every Thursday. There is also a famous pole to climb when you have the urge (and Dutch courage) to write your name on the roof.

Jo'burg

218 Long Street; tel: 021 422 0142; www.joburgbar.com; Mon–Sat noon–late, Sun 8pm–late; map p.136 A2

Find yourself among a colourful crowd of South Africans and foreign backpackers. Stand toe-to-toe with the boozers at the bar, take a booth and people-watch or spill out onto the street in summer when the temperature rises.

Long Street Café

259 Long Street; tel: 021 424 2464; Mon–Sat 9.30am–1am; map p.136 A3

Though it's faded a bit over the years when compared to some of the newer arrivals and other competitors that

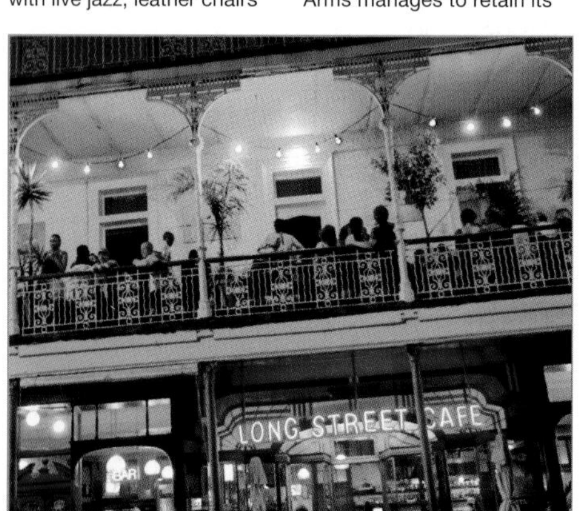

Left: the ever-popular Long Street Café.

Left: Jo'burg in the City Centre.

Most bars will let you run a tab with the deposit of your credit card behind the bar; just remember to sign off with a reasonable tip for the barman – they have a good memory when it comes to that sort of thing.

have refurbished, upgraded and reinvented themselves, Long Street Café is still a decent enough spot. It offers cocktails (try the Long Street iced tea), a light menu, lounge chairs and a good street-level vantage point from which to plan your next move into the night.

Mercury Live
43 De Villiers Street, Zonnebloem; tel: 021 465 2106; www.mercuryl.co.za; Wed–Sat 8pm–4am; map p.136 B4
One of Cape Town's oldest live-music venues and popular bar hangouts, Mercury Live attracts a steady stream of musos and fans. From rock to punk and back again, this joint is gritty rather than pretty but the drinks are cheap, the music loud, the hours long and the experience consistent.

Mr Pickwick's
158 Long Street; tel: 021 423 3710; Mon–Sat 8am–1am; map p.136 A2
Reliably dark and dingy and unpretentious – which is how both tourists and locals like it – Mr Pickwick's is a Long Street institution. Part coffee and sandwich shop, part bar and lounge, the patrons are tattooed, hairy, relaxed and often foreign. Worth a visit if only for the milkshakes or the morning-after breakfasts.

Neighbourhood Bar and Restaurant
163 Long Street; tel: 021 424 7260; Mon–Thur 4pm until late, Fri–Sat 2pm until late; map p.136 A2
The atmosphere and décor creates a comfortable mix somewhere between someone's living room, a library and a bar, leaving you feeling at home in no time. With live-music nights, pub quiz, a wide beer selection, a bar counter made from vintage watch parts and a balcony from which to watch the ever-changing scene on Long Street, it's rapidly become a firm favourite.

The Waiting Room
273 Long Street Cape Town; tel: 021 422 4536; Mon–Sat 6pm–2am; map p.136 A3
A chilled hipster hangout spot perched high above Cape Town's nightlife centre of Long Street, The Waiting Room offers a great buzz, a cool crowd and both resident DJs and local bands playing small sets. Have dinner downstairs in its sister establishment, **Royale Eatery** *(see p.105)*, and then work your way up through the warren of stairs and alcoves to the viewing deck looking over Long Street. A good starting point for your night out.

Zula Sound Bar
196 Long Street; tel: 021 424 2442; www.zulabar.co.za; daily 12am–late; map p.136 A2
With live music, theatre, stand-up comedy and performance poetry, affordable booze, less attitude than any of the neighbouring Long Street bars and a cosmopolitan crowd, Zula has all the ingredients for a different night out. There's also a pool and table-football room for those with twitchy thumbs.

City Bowl

Asoka
68 Kloof Street, Gardens; tel: 021 422 0909; www.asokabar.co.za; daily 5pm–2am; map p.135 E4
This sophisticated cocktail and tapas bar sports good food, chill-out DJs and an interesting aesthetic aspect in that a tree grows out of the middle of the space. Get in by 10pm, as after that it's difficult to find standing room, let alone seats.

Carlyles on Derry
17 Derry Street, Vredehoek; tel: 021 461 8787; Tue–Sun 5.30–late; map p.136 B4

Offering excellent pizza, legendary lamb shanks, a bar with a buzz and a legion of people who consider it not only their local, but their kitchen, this cosy Vredehoek spot is packed night in, night out. One of the least pretentious and most cheerful places to go for a relaxed drink, comfort food and a conversation you can actually hear.

Caveau Wine Bar and Deli
Heritage Square, 92 Bree Street; tel: 021 422 1367; www.caveau.co.za; Mon–Sat 7am–10.30pm; map p.136 A2
With excellent food (both deli and à la carte), discreet, knowledgeable service, an extensive wine list and a wonderfully cosy atmosphere, Caveau is a favourite amongst the Cape's foodies, wine-lovers and anyone who enjoys a combination of the two. While cosy in winter, it's very sociable in summer, with outside seating on historic Bree Street. The success of this establishment has led to the opening of a sister establishment in Newlands *(see p.33)*. Try the off-menu steak tartare and ribbon fries.

Planet Champagne Bar
Mount Nelson Hotel, 76 Orange Street; tel: 021 483 1000; www.mountnelson.co.za; daily 5pm–late; map p.135 E3
While the Mount Nelson *(see p.63)*, or Nellie (the grande dame of Cape Town's hotels) is all about old money, the Planet Champagne Bar is a lot more accessible while remaining a five-star bar. Choose from a wide selection of wines, French champagnes and cocktails, and get comfortable either in the well-appointed lounge under the twinkling fibre-optic Milky Way ceiling display or on the balcony looking over the Nellie's manicured lawns.

Rafiki's
13B Kloof Nek Road, Tamboerskloof; tel: 021 426 4731; daily 9am–12pm; map p.139 D1
Big-screen TVs for sport, a generous prawn special, waitresses with a delightfully uninterested attitude and some dodgy unisex bathrooms. This one's a favourite with locals who come to watch the workers slog home and the sun disappear between Lion's Head and Signal Hill.

Rick's Café Americain
2 Park Road, Gardens; tel: 021 424 1100; Mon–Sat 11.30am–2am; map p.137 D4
Housed in a renovated cottage just off busy Kloof Street and not far from the entertainment epicentre of Long Street, Rick's is an excellent option for drinks (they've got a solid wine list), tapas (theirs is a Mediterranean/North African-influenced menu) and, in summer, drinks on the deck upstairs. It's popular with the moneyed late 20s/early 30s crowd looking for after-work drinks to take the edge off another hard day in the Mother City.

Relish
70 New Church Street, Tamboerskloof; tel: 021 422 3584; www.relish.co.za; Mon–Fri 12pm–late, Sat 5pm–late; map p.135 E3
The amazing views of Table Mountain from this three-storey bar/gastro-pub stuck to the side of busy Kloof Nek Road make it worth the visit alone, but the pizzas and cocktail list are also highlights. Frequented by the thirsty after-work crowd. If

you get carried away, stay at the neighbouring Protea Fire and Ice Hotel *(see p.63)*.

Victoria and Alfred Waterfront

Bascule
The Cape Grace Hotel, West Quay Road; tel: 021 410 7082; www.capegrace.com; daily 9am–2am; map p.133 E3
South Africa's premier whisky bar (over 460 types on offer at last count) is set in a cosy cellar under **The Cape Grace Hotel** *(see p.64)*. Enjoy views of Table Mountain while seals bark at you from the nearby harbour. It's frequented by moneyed business folk and the kinds of people who step off the mega-yachts moored in the marina. Live music on a Wednesday.

Buena Vista Social Café
81 Main Road, 1st Floor Exhibition House, Green Point; tel: 021 433 0611; Mon–Sun 12am–late; map p.133 C3
From the faded paintwork to the rickety wooden furniture and the ubiquitous Che and Fidel paraphernalia, this Cuban-themed restaurant/bar does well with a tired theme and leaves you feeling as though you could've been hanging with the guerrillas prior to invading Havana. Order a few chilli poppers off the starter menu or puff away on one of the big-brand Cuban cigars on offer.

Cubana
9 Somerset Road, De Waterkant Centre, Green Point; tel: 021 421 1109; Mon–Sat 8am–late, Sun 10am–late; map p.133 D4
The town instalment of this successful Cuban-themed chain has a dance floor, a large bar, plenty of booths, a pseudo-Mediterranean/South American menu and bouncers with attitude. In truth, this is Cuba-lite and more of a party spot and pick-up joint than anything else.

Mitchell's Ale House
East Pier Head; tel: 021 419 5074; daily 11am–1.30am; map p.133 E2
This is an old-fashioned working man's pub in the heart of the Waterfront. Beer brewed on the site adds to the appeal of this establishment. Right next door is **Ferryman's** pub where you can also grab a bite to eat after a few stouts.

Paulaner Brauhaus Shop 18
Piazza Level, Clock Tower Square, V&A Waterfront; tel: 021 418 9999; daily 11am–11.30pm; map p.133 E3
Connected to the Munich brewery of the same name which has been around since 1634, the Cape Town branch (there are other outlets in Singapore and Beijing) also brews its own beer on the premises. Popular with European tourists and anyone else chasing fantastic beer, Wiener schnitzel and eisbein, this is good at what it does but is not for visitors who like to avoid other tourists. It is, however, very convenient if you're fresh off the Robben Island Ferry and thirsty.

Southern Suburbs

Caveau at The Mill
13 Boundary Road, Josephine's Mill, Newlands; tel: 021 685 6140; www.caveau.co.za; Mon–Sat 7am–12pm;

> Hotel bars tend to offer cool sophistication at a price, whilst Long Street in the City Centre has a more bohemian feel to them. The suburbs are dotted with old-fashioned pubs that are good for beer and sport, or wherever the mood takes you.

Left: Caveau Wine Bar and Deli.

Left: great views from Relish.

map p.133 D4
The sister establishment to the popular **Caveau Wine Bar and Deli** *(see p.32)*, Caveau Newlands is wedged between Newlands rugby stadium and the Liesbeeck River in a historic old mill. Caveau's focus points of an extensive wine list, excellent food and efficient service are maintained.

The Forrester's Arms
51 Newlands Avenue; tel: 021 689 5949; Mon–Sat 11am–11pm, Sun 11am–6pm
A popular English-style pub in the leafy suburb of Newlands, The Forrester's Arms (or Forries as it is known to regulars, who consist of anyone from university students to professionals) serves great pub grub, has a wide selection of beer on tap, and is dotted with TVs for big sporting events. However, the best thing about Forries is probably the beer garden. There is also a children's play area.

Oblivion
22 Chichester Road, Corner of 3rd Street and Chichester Road, Harfield Village; tel: 021 671 8522; daily 11.30am–3am
This wine bar with comfortable leather couches, open fires, board games, massive glasses of wine and snack fare is one of the Southern Suburbs' few real night-out destinations. It starts as a destination for relaxed post-work drinks and transforms into a dance club halfway through the evening, as tables and chairs are cleared and the lit-up dance floor starts to flash. No under-23s.

For those wanting something a little quieter (and perhaps more romantic), head to the Twelve Apostles Hotel's **Leopard Bar** overlooking the Atlantic Ocean. It has an impressive list of over 72 (rather potent) Martini cocktails and a variety of flavoured vodkas. Enjoy live entertainment every Mon–Wed and Fri evening. Great complimentary bar snacks to nibble on too. *See also Hotels, p.66.*

Constantia Valley

The Martini
The Cellars-Hohenhort, 93 Brommersvlei Road, Constantia; tel: 021 794 2137; www.collectionmcgrath.com; daily 7am–11.30pm
This sexy little cocktail bar inside this old-world hotel is where you can expect to find Cape Town's most extensive Martini menu, with over 152 different types to choose from. A perfect spot to meet for a drink during the week, where you can dress up for the occasion too.

Atlantic Seaboard and Cape Peninsula

Baraza
The Promenade, Victoria Road, Camps Bay; tel: 021 438 2016; daily 12am–late; map p.138 A3
One of the many beach bar/lounge options on Camps Bay's Victoria Road strip, Zanzibar-inspired Baraza means 'street place' in Swahili. It's more chi-chi than that implies and offers extra, in that along with the beautiful bodies fresh off the beach and the offerings of a well-stocked bar, there are often decent DJs playing afro-chill-out tunes.

Café Caprice
37 Victoria Road, Camps Bay, 8001; tel: 021 438 8315; www.cafecaprice.co.za; daily 9am–late; map p.138 A3
Crowded and cool, Cape Town's premier beach bar

Right: the beer garden at The Forrester's Arms.

Left: a cosy corner at The Martini.

along Camps Bay's main strip is one of the ultimate see-and-be-seen destinations in Cape Town. Go there for post-beach sundowners or drinks to get your evening started and expect to bump into celebs and plenty of models.

La Med

Glen Country Club, Victoria Road, Clifton; tel: 021 438 5600; Mon–Fri 11am–late, Sat–Sun, 9am–late; map p.138 A2

Best spot for sundowners. With little in front of it save for a cricket field and the boulders holding back the waves, La Med in Camps Bay seems to have been around forever and a day, and is the perfect place to watch the sun disappear over the Atlantic in summer. In winter it's popular for catching sport on its big screens. Service is slow. Cover charge applies in summer, and parking in the adjacent parking lot has become a rip-off of late. If you're driving, better to park on Victoria Road.

The Nag's Head

Village Lane, Chapmans Peak; tel: 021 789 2973; www.nagshead.co.za

After taking in the sights of the Peninsula from Cape Point to Hout Bay, The Nag's Head is an attractive option. With a bar upstairs and a restaurant serving conventional pub grub downstairs, you can slake a thirst or satiate your hunger pangs with a substantial feed.

The Red Herring

Corner of Beach and Pine roads, Noordhoek; tel: 021 789 1783; Tue–Sun 6.30–10pm

Forget Route 66 and the south of France, Chapman's Peak is arguably the world's most beautiful drive. Winding around from Hout Bay with views towards the bay, Dungeons surf spot (where the Red Bull Big Wave Africa takes place) and the Sentinel peak, your car sticks to the dramatic cliff road protected by boulder nets. Once you've made it over to the Noordhoek side of the drive, The Red Herring is where you go for draught beer and some of the best pizzas in town.

Sandbar

31 Victoria Road, Camps Bay; tel: 021 438 8336; www.sandbar.co.za; Mon–Sun 9.30am–late; map p.138 A3

Employing the effective recipe of cocktails, a relaxed dress code and street-side tables where patrons can see and be seen, Sandbar is a stone's throw across Victoria (and the passing Ferraris) from Camps Bay beach. Perfect for when you're feeling parched after a day on the beach.

Tobagos

Radisson SAS Hotel, Beach Road, Granger Bay; tel: 021 441 3000; www.radissonsas.com; 24 hours; map p.133 D2

Here on Friday nights after work (mostly during the summer season) is where most Capetonians meet to cool off after a busy week with a couple of drinks. Drinks don't come cheap and the service can be exceptionally slow, but the views and lapping waves only metres away make it all worth the wait.

Wafu/Wakame

2nd floor, Corner of Beach Road and Surrey Place, Mouille Point; tel: 021 433 2377/434 5134; www.wakame.co.za; Sun–Mon 12am–10.30pm; map p.132 C2

Perched above its sister restaurant Wakame in Mouille Point adjacent to the V&A Waterfront, Wafu is one of the best places in Cape Town to go for tapas and sundowners (Robben Island where Nelson Mandela was imprisoned makes up part of the view). Sleek wooden fittings, an aquarium for the bar and an elegant crowd complete the make-up of this smart coastal bar. Try the chilli and lime calamari off the dim sum menu.

Beaches

Around the Cape's fynbos-covered coastline are coves, inlets and sandy beaches popular with the locals, not for swimming because the water is mostly far too cold, but for surfing, sunbathing or dog-walking. The Atlantic Seaboard from Sea Point to Camps Bay is very built up, and beautiful bodies bathe at Clifton near some of the most expensive real estate in Africa. The False Bay coast is much warmer than the Atlantic Seaboard all the way to Hout Bay. At Fish Hoek, St James and Muizenberg you can swim for hours, only there are a few Great white sharks that lurk in the deeper waters beyond, so stay close to the shore.

Boulders Beach

Kleintuin Road, Simon's Town, Atlantic Seaboard; tel: 021 786 2329; www.tmnp.co.za; entrance charge

Well known for its rare jackass penguins (also known as African penguins) which colonised the beach in 1982, Boulders Beach is now a national park. The beach is magnificent and offers a protected cove for swimming. Should you want to see the penguins, you'll have to buy a pass from the kiosk, then walk along specially constructed boardwalks where you can get up close to them.

Camps Bay

Victoria Road, Camps Bay, Atlantic Seaboard; map p.138 A3

Beneath the majestic Twelve Apostles mountain range, this world-famous white stretch of beach is one of the hippest hangouts for any keen beach-goer. Think palm trees, pebble-smooth boulders propped up in the sand (where you can often find a quiet, protected spot from the wind), turquoise waters and a line-up of trendy eateries and cafés that stay open long after dark. It offers easy access and a few rock pools to the left of the beach (if you're facing the ocean), which is a safer swimming alternative for those with smaller children.

Traffic is chaotic over the festive season and parking is limited, but it is possible to find a space in the residential areas, monitored by security guards, and take a stroll

Left: Clifton's Second Beach.

Left: the boulder-strewn beach at Camps Bay.

Secret Beaches

Beta Beach: take Victoria Road into Beta Road and follow the path to the north or south side. Beta is a secluded cove that looks up at Lion's Head, covered in crushed seashells and perfect for catching a tan without the crowds eyeing you out.
Clifton Fifth: follow the M6 southbound from Sea Point. A tiny spot of beach to the south of Clifton Fourth Beach. It's a little more rocky than it is sandy, but it's the perfect spot for a sundowner or a romantic full-moon picnic.
Diaz Beach: Cape of Good Hope Nature Reserve. This is one of the most beautiful and isolated beaches you'll ever see. Because of this, don't go alone and beware of the baboons living in the area. Take a steep path down to the beach from the car park at the end of Cape Point road. It's worth every drop of sweat and tears you will endure on the way up and down.
Glen Beach: Next to Camps Bay, north towards Clifton. A popular spot for surfers, this small enclave of protected beach is perfect for those wanting time out from the holidaying crowds, but still close to the main strip of Camps Bay with a choice of foodie restaurants and bars that will keep you going into the early hours of the morning.

Left: Boulders Beach.

down to the beach. Loungers and umbrellas are available for rent; a personal masseuse is on hand should you require some de-stressing.

Clifton

Victoria Road, Atlantic Seaboard; map p.134 A3/138 A1

Clifton has four little wind-free coves divided by boulders, each one an amphitheatre lined with upmarket beach bungalows. All of them reached from the road down winding steep steps, **Fourth Beach**, the furthest away, is longer and wider than the others and generally packed with young families. It's safe to bathe here if you can bear the icy waters. Next-door **Third Beach** is where you'll find the most beautiful bodies in town. Popular with gay men, this is the place to be and be seen. At **Second Beach** you'll find quieter couples lazing under their umbrellas after a game of Frisbee. **First Beach** is much the same but less busy. You must also climb up more than 100 steps to get back to your car, which in the heat of summer is quite a feat. A little further offshore there are always several private yachts anchored in the bay, and for the active there is water-skiing and canoeing on offer. Loungers, beach umbrellas and cool refreshments are readily available. Just lie back and relax.

Fish Hoek and Clovelly Beach

Fish Hoek (enter at the boom on the Fish Hoek end, or park at the parking area as you enter Fish Hoek on the Clovelly side), Atlantic Seaboard

Beyond Simon's Town, the M4 meanders around the coast through Glencairn to Fish Hoek. The family-friendly swimming beach is cut off from the town by a railway line and poor development, but you'll be pleasantly

surprised how fun a day spent on the sand and in the warm waves can be. There is also a safe playground area and a restaurant serving delicious ice lollies. **Clovelly Beach** is popular amongst beginner surfers and body-boarders. It has been long been considered quite an eccentric town, ever since a law in 1818 decreed that public ale houses were banned from the original farmstead. Today Fish Hoek still doesn't have have a single liquor store.

Llandudno

Victoria Road, Atlantic Seaboard
As you come along Victoria Road towards Hout Bay you'll corkscrew your way down to Llandudno beach. This is another expensive suburb of stylish (and some not-so-stylish) beach houses built right up against the mountainside to maximise the panoramic ocean views. Tucked amongst boulders, providing some excellent shelter from the pumping southeasterly wind, Llandudno is a casual, family beach, popular amongst young and older surfers. There are no shops in Llandudno, so remember to pack a light picnic for the day. The small parking lot above the beach fills up very quickly over high season, so be prepared to park and walk down from one of the side streets.

Noordhoek Beach

Kommetjie, Atlantic Seaboard
As you come around the final bend of Chapman's Peak Drive from Hout Bay, look straight ahead and you will see Noordhoek Beach, which runs for about 6km (4 miles). The perfect spot for horse-riding, its natural wetlands also attract a wonderful variety of birds and indigenous wildlife. It is now owned by South African National Parks to ensure its future protec-

Left: colourful beach huts at St James beach. **Right:** the Atlantic Seaboard has plenty of beaches to choose from.

tion. There are also a few shipwrecks to be seen in the sand. However, the isolation of this beautiful spot has attracted muggers over the years, so leave your valuables at home and tell someone where you are going before you leave.

St James and Muizenberg Beach

Park near St James Station, then go through the tunnel running under the railway line, Atlantic Seaboard

Kalk Bay runs into **St James**, which is another pretty seaside village. Victorian villas line the seafront, with cobbled alleyways linking houses and shops on the slope beneath St James's Peak. There are lovely warm tidal pools that flank the shore, its calm waters perfect for those wanting to lull in the water. You can't miss the multi-coloured beach huts which line this tiny beach.

St James merges with **Muizenberg** a little further down the road. Here the coastline boasts a sweep of beach that heads towards Gordon's Bay, 25km (15 miles) away. The water is safe for swimming and the temperature is relatively warm, and it is a favourite surf spot for first-timers and those more advanced. Muizenberg has long been a favourite beach for Capetonians, ever since 1882 when the railway was built and people came here in droves to enjoy the warm waters.

Sandy Bay

Follow the signs from Llandudno, off Victoria Road, Atlantic Seaboard

If you take a 15-minute walk from Llandudno, discover Cape Town's unofficial nudist beach, secluded by huge boulders and little private inlets and overhangs. The only way to reach Sandy Bay is to park in the small area at the end of the road, then walk for about 3km (2 miles) along the long white beach with enormous protected sand dunes. This unspoilt beach is popular with couples, same-sex and straight, who make a day of it as the walk to get there is quite long. Take an umbrella and cool-box with food and drinks. Dogs are welcome, too.

Sea Point Promenade

Beach Road, Sea Point, Atlantic Seaboard; map p.132 A3/134 B1

Just below this grassy seaside strip alive with joggers, dog-walkers, lovers and children playing, you will find the occasional stretch of beach where you can swim in some old tidal pools, which at the weekend are very busy indeed. Graaff's Pool is a wide natural rock pool protected from view by a whitewashed wall, which is a nudist haven in the heart of the city. Gay men cruise the area until the early hours of the morning. The newly restored Sea Point Public Pool is set right on the ocean with an Olympic-sized pool (and kiddies' splash pool) complete with changing rooms and showers.

Right: Llandudno.

Children

If you're worried about entertaining your kids during your trip, you'll be pleased to know that Cape Town is full of ideas when it comes to catering for children of all ages. Some natural encounters include time with camels, sharks and ostriches. However, there's always the planetarium at the Iziko South African Museum, digging for colourful gems at the Scratch Patch or a wild rollercoaster ride at the Ratanga Junction theme park for those who are a little older. Small children are granted free access to most attractions, and the city is generally child-friendly, but we've also listed a few child-specific eateries.

Imhoff Farm, Kommetjie

Kommetjie Road, Kommetjie, Atlantic Seaboard; tel: 021 783 4545; www.imhofffarm.co.za; daily 10am–5pm

Here there is a complete farmyard, snake park, horse-riding and camel rides on the beach. A one-stop shop for child-friendly activities (especially if you are on your way to the Cape Point Nature Reserve).

Iziko South African Museum

25 Queen Victoria Street, City Centre; tel: 021 481 3800/3900; www.iziko.org.za/sam; museum: daily 10am–5pm, planetarium shows: Mon–Fri 2pm, Tue 8pm, Sat–Sun noon, 1pm, 2.30pm; entrance charge; map p.136 A3

An up-to-the-minute museum that consistently offers detailed, fun-filled exhibits. The Whale Well is always a hit with children, although the dinosaurs are quite terrifying and very real-looking.

PLANETARIUM

Sit inside a dark room and watch the night sky appear before your eyes. A variety of shows cater for all age groups where they attempt to answer questions, like 'Why is the sky blue?' and 'Is the sun round?' The Twinkle Show is a playful introduction to astronomy especially for the under-10s and is just right for enquiring young minds. To get there, take a stroll along Government Avenue.

SEE ALSO MUSEUMS AND GALLERIES, P.78

Monkey Town

Mondeor Road, Somerset West; tel: 021 858 1060; www.monkeys.co.za; daily 9am–5pm; entrance charge

Feel like aping around? Monkey Town is a primate paradise home to 25 simian species, from chimpanzees to curious lemurs and vervet monkeys. Excellent supervised holiday programmes and interactive sessions with the simians are available.

Ratanga Junction

Century Boulevard, Century City, Sable Street exit, N1; tel: 086 120 0300; www.ratanga.co.za; open during major school holidays, summer daily 10am–6pm; entrance charge

The one and only theme park in Cape Town that tends to go into hibernation over the win-

Left: feeding the seals at Two Oceans Aquarium.

Left: Two Oceans Aquarium.

Kid-Friendly Restaurants

Deer Park Café, 2 Deer Park Drive, Highlands Estate, Vredehoek, City Bowl; tel: 021 462 6311; daily 8am–8pm. Attached to a public park, local mums and dads gather here for the healthy kiddies' menu, wide open spaces and fresh mountain air.

Café Roux, Noordhoek Farm Village, Noordhoek; tel: 021 789 2538; www.caferoux.co.za; Tue–Sun 8.30am–11.15am, noon–3.30pm. A favourite weekend spot where your kids and even your dogs get royal treatment. Separate kiddies' menu available.

The Barnyard Farmstall, 4 Steenberg Road, Steenberg; tel: 021 712 6934; Mon–Fri 8.30am–4.30pm, Sat–Sun 9am–5pm. Wholesome country fare in a charming location at the foot of the Ou Kaapseweg mountain pass. There is a small farmyard of animals.

ter months. Enjoy a thrilling ride like The Cobra, The Slingshot or The Diamond Devil Run. More sedate family rides are also available.

Scratch Patch

Dock Road, V&A Waterfront; tel: 021 419 9429; www.scratchpatch.co.za; daily 9am–5.30am; map p.133 D3

The two Scratch Patches (one at the V&A Waterfront and the other in Simon's Town) are the perfect place for treasure-seekers to crawl around in a pit of multi-coloured pebbles and semi-precious stones. Look out for a Tiger's Eye and pretty Rose Quartz. Prices range from R12 for a small bag to R65 for a large container.

(Also at: Dido Valley Road, Simon's Town; tel: 021 786 2020; Mon–Fri 8.30am–4.45pm)

Spier Wine Estate, Stellenbosch

R310, Lynedoch Area, Stellenbosch; tel: 021 809 1100; www.spier.co.za; daily 10am–5pm

The ideal outdoor entertainment venue for kids of all ages. It's quite a drive out of town to Stellenbosch, but once you get there, it's an entertainment playground. The on-site attractions include the Cheetah Outreach, which offers the rare opportunity to interact with the cheetahs, and the Eagle Outreach explores different birds of prey. There is also a large picnic area with a restaurant and deli and wine-tasting for weary parents.

Stadium on Main

Main Road, Claremont; tel: 021 671 3665; daily 8.30am–midnight

Apart from the bowling alley downstairs, this small shopping mall has a rooftop entertaining area featuring action cricket, netball and beach volleyball. Social and league games throughout the week.

Two Oceans Aquarium

Dock Road, V&A Waterfront; tel: 021 418 3823; www.aquarium.co.za; daily 9.30am–6pm; free; map p.133 E3

This is a must-visit for all children (and adults). Highlights include the predator tank, where you can watch ragged-tooth sharks and stingrays circulate, the mesmerising Kelp Forest, and a family of playful Cape seals ducking and diving on the basement level. There is also a touch pool where kids can prod and poke a variety of anemones and sea urchins.

World of Birds

Valley Road, Hout Bay; tel: 021 790 2730; www.worldofbirds.org.za; daily 9am–5pm; entrance charge

Africa's largest bird park boasts walk-through aviaries containing more than 3,000 birds and small animals ranging from peacocks to lovebirds and flamingos. The average visit takes between three and four hours, so you may want to set aside half a day for this family excursion.

Churches, Synagogues and Mosques

Most South Africans are Christians, the largest denominations being Anglican (Church of England), Roman Catholic and Dutch Reformed. There are also large Jewish and Muslim communities living in the Western Cape. Here we've noted some of the most historically important or architecturally striking places of worship that can be explored on foot or by private tour.

Auwal Mosque

43 Dorp Street, Bo-Kaap; tel: 021 422 1671; by appointment only; map p.136 A2

A political prisoner and prince from the Indonesian island Tidore, Tuan Guru established the country's first *masjid* on land donated by Saartjie van de Kaap, the daughter of a freed slave. Situated on the cobbled streets of the Bo-Kaap, it is considered one of the country's oldest mosques and dates from between 1785 and 1798. It is also believed to be the place where the Afrikaans language was first studied. Today it continues to play an integral part in the community.

Dutch Reformed Church

39 Upper Adderley Street, City Centre; tel: 021 422 0569; www.grootekerk.org.za; Mon–Fri 10am–2pm, Sunday Services 10am, 7pm; map p.136 B2

Also known as **Die Groote Kerk**, this imposing square structure looks nothing like a church from its exterior, even though it's one of the oldest in the country. Take a step inside and be inspired by the impressive domed ceiling unsupported by pillars, and the giant organ or the pulpit carved by master sculptor Anton Anreith and carpenter Jacob Graaf, which sits on the shoulders of two feisty-looking lions. A crypt underneath the church is the resting place of several governors of the Cape, among them Simon van der Stel.

> Whilst designing the interiors of the Groote Kerk, Anreith envisioned the three Virgins (Faith, Hope and Charity) occupying the space around the pulpit, but the Church Council denied his request, claiming the sculptured bodies of the women were too scantily clad.

Great Synagogue

88 Hatfield Street, Gardens, entry via Jewish Museum gate; tel: 021 465 1405; www.gardensshul.org; Mon–Thur, every 2nd Sun; free; map p.136 A3

This is South Africa's mother synagogue, designed in the style of Central European Baroque churches with a big dome and two towers on either side. Better-known as the Gardens Shul, the interior is adorned with stained-glass windows and gold-leaf mosaic friezes. It can also seat up to 1,400 people. The oldest-built synagogue, known as the Old Shul, is situated next door and is part of the **Jewish Museum**.

SEE ALSO MUSEUMS AND GALLERIES, P.79

Lutheran Church

98 Strand Street, City Centre: tel: 021 421 5854; Mon–Fri 10am–2pm, Sun 10am service; map p.136 A1

Neighbouring the Gold of Africa Museum *(see p.77)*, the Lutheran Church, an old barn in its early days, was converted by Anton Anreith. The interior is filled with late-18th-century and early-19th-century decorative art. Like the Groote Kerk, it has an Anreith-designed pulpit and lectern and one of the few surviving 18th-century street frontages.

Right: the towers of the Great Synagogue and St Georges Cathedral.

Left: the Dutch Reformed Church (Die Groot Kerk).

Metropolitan Methodist Church

Greenmarket Square, Corner of Longmarket and Burg streets, City Centre; tel: 021 422 2744; Mon–Fri 9am–2pm, Sat 10am–noon; free; map p.136 A2

Regarded as one of the finest places of worship in the country, this historic Gothic structure with its tall spire reaching towards the sky and pointed arches is situated right in the middle of buzzing Greenmarket Square, and dwarfed by most of the surrounding buildings. It also houses a small exhibit on the history of the old Methodist Church in Buitenkant Street (now the **District Six Museum**, *see p.77*) which was a safe haven for political activists during the Apartheid years.

Palm Tree Mosque

185 Long Street, City Centre; not open to the public; map p.136 A2

Flanked by palm trees, the second-oldest mosque in Cape Town is wedged between a bar and a Gothic-style fashion boutique. Established by Jan van Boughies, a freed slave who created a small prayer room that over the years slowly developed into fully fledged and extremely popular mosque.

St Georges Cathedral

5 Wale Street, City Centre; tel: 021 424 7360; www.stgeorgescathedral.com; Mon–Fri 8.30am–4.30pm; free; map p.136 A2

South Africa's oldest cathedral, also dubbed 'The People's Cathedral' because it remained open to all races throughout the Apartheid years. In the past its pews were regularly packed with protestors addressed by the first black Archbishop of Cape Town, Desmond Tutu. The church is worth a visit just to admire the beautiful stained-glass windows or a walk around the courtyard with its labyrinth.

South African Slave Church Museum

40 Long Street, City Centre; tel: 021 423 6755; Mon–Fri 9am–4pm, school holidays 9am–noon; free; map p.136 B1

This small building, which if you blink once you might miss it, is home to the Cape's first slave church, built in 1804. An ongoing exhibition at the museum focuses on the Christian religion, which had an enormous influence on the slave community and other indigenous ethnic groups.

Environment

Cape Town's unique environment is also its greatest asset, making it one of the most desirable places in the world to live, work and play, over and above being a sought-after tourist destination. Located within the Cape Floral Kingdom, the city is not only a thriving economic hub but also a biodiversity hot spot of international importance. With the recent implementation of the City's Integrated Metropolitan Environmental Policy, key areas of managing sustainability include biodiversity issues, energy and climate change, coastal management, as well as environmental education training.

Cape Floral Kingdom

The Cape is recognised as the smallest of the world's six recognised floral kingdoms, an ecological island that extends over some 90,000sq km (3,475sq miles) yet supports a total of almost 9,000 flowering plant species, including numerous bulbs, heathers, grasses and proteas, most of which occur nowhere else in the world. Locally these plants are known as fynbos because they have hardy wooden stems and fine leaves. In general they grow low to the ground and are extremely well adapted to high winds, long droughts, fire and wet, cool winters.

Fynbos Conservation

Large parts of the fynbos region have been developed for agriculture or through the urban expansion around Cape Town. Fynbos areas are also threatened by the spread of alien species, in particular wattle and acacia species from Australia, as well as pine plantations. Many species have become extinct, and more than 1,000 are endangered. Their conservation is a priority, and reserves have been established in many areas to protect their unique natural heritage in a modern environment.

Biodiversity Challenges

The City of Cape Town has joined an international initiative called **Local Action for Biodiversity** (LAB), focusing on strategies to protect and develop biodiversity – a diversity of plant and animal life – as a natural resource within municipalities. Key issues include the destruction of endangered habitat – through conversion to agriculture and rapid urbanisation – as the primary threat to the city's biodiversity management plans. Other primary challenges include managing invasive vegetation, climate change, poor communication and lack of capacity (LAB Project, 44 Wale Street, Cape Town; tel: 021 487 2070; www.iclei.org).

Green Travel

Low-cost local airline company **Kulula.com** has over the last few years intro-

Left and below: members of the Cape Floral Kingdom.

Straw-bale homes are a growing (and economically attractive) architecture trend in South Africa, and in particular Cape Town. The bale construction uses baled straw from wheat, oats, barley, rye, rice and others in walls covered by stucco. This technique for constructing walls has been recently revived as a low-cost alternative for building highly insulating walls as well as good for the environment. For more details contact Eco Design Architects, tel: 021 462 1614; www.ecodesignarchitects.co.za, who are leading the way in this field.

duced a fleet of more fuel-efficient and planet-friendly planes. It is also part of a green initiative together with **Food & Trees for Africa** that targets the planting of 1,000 trees before the end of 2008 in new and deteriorated developments, including landscaping projects at school playgrounds and township communities. For further details visit www.kulula.co.za.

Energy Crisis

Eskom's (South African Electricity Supply Company) system of rotating existing power supplies, better-known as load-shedding, looks to be with the country for between five and seven years while systems are upgraded to cope with increased demand.

Over the past decade, South Africa has experienced a steady growth in the demand for electricity linked to increased economic growth. This has exhausted Eskom's surplus electricity-generation capacity and reduced the reserve margin progressively. In response, it has accelerated the implementation of its capacity expansion programme and will invest R150 billion in the upgrading of the country's power-supply infrastructure. The City of Cape Town also recently signed a 20-year power purchase agreement with a wind energy producer in Darling, a small town north west of Cape Town, that will generate an estimated 13.2 gigawatt-hours per year of 'clean' electricity.

All major hotels, shopping malls and most restaurants in the City Centre have generators so most visitors won't be left in the dark.

Essentials

Cape Town is a very easy city to navigate and negotiate. Here is all the information you will need to understand issues such as currency, who to call in an emergency, and where to find the closest tourist office. There are also details on embassies, business hours, telephone services and health care. For additional information visit www.cape-town.org, or gather a few useful tips at the Cape Town tourism desk at the airport on arrival. For the weather forecast bureau, tel: 082-231 1640; www.weathersa.co.za, or consult the daily newspapers. For details on how to get around the city, *see also Transport, p.124–5.*

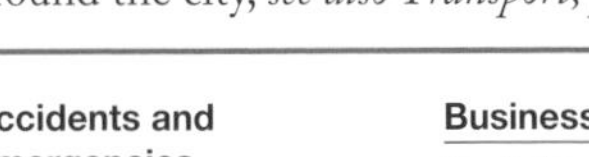

Accidents and Emergencies

Cape Town offers an extensive range of high-standard public and private hospitals. It's recommended that tourists go to a private hospital to be treated, as there are usually more doctors to go around. It is highly advisable to take out travel insurance for the duration of your trip, because in the event of an accident this should help cover your medical expenses.

Business Hours

Most shops in the city and the suburbs are open 9am–5pm on weekdays and until 1pm on Saturdays. All activity comes to a halt at 1pm on Saturdays in the City Centre. However, shopping malls like the V&A Waterfront, Cavendish Square in Claremont and Canal Walk at Century City stay open from 9am–9pm throughout the week (10am Sunday). Government agencies are open Mon–Fri 9am–5pm. Muslim-owned businesses close noon–1pm on Fridays for prayers. Most liquor stores close at 6pm (Mon–Sat). Supermarkets generally close at 6pm during the week, 5pm on Saturday and until 2pm on Sundays.

Clothing

What to pack? Cape Town is generally informal when it comes to what to wear, particularly in summer. That said, most businessmen will wear a suit and tie except on hot

Left: Cape Town parking attendants.

Emergency Services tel: 10177
Netcare tel: 911/ 082 911
General emergencies tel: 107 (from a landline) or 112 from a mobile phone
Mountain Rescue Services tel: 021 873 1121; 021 948 9900
Poison Crisis Centre tel: 021 931 6129
Police tel: 10111
Red Cross Children's Hospital tel: 021 658 5111
National Sea Rescue Institute tel: 021 449 3500.

days, when it is acceptable to go without a jacket. These days, for an informal lunch or shopping expedition you can get away with wearing casual shorts and T-shirts.

In the evening most restaurants expect smart-casual dress, but more exclusive places prefer men to wear a jacket and tie.

It rains quite often in Cape Town between May and August, so bring a raincoat. Summers are long and dry, which calls for light clothing and a swimsuit, but bring a warm jacket or sweater for trips up Table Mountain, boat trips or for travelling around the Peninsula.

Consulates

Most of the major consulates and embassies are situated in Johannesburg, but several countries do have representatives or consulates in Cape Town. If your consulate isn't listed below, consult the Yellow Pages or call Directory Enquiries (tel: 1023).

Left: some Capetonians take security *very* seriously.

Austrian Consulate
1 Thibault Square, Cape Town; tel: 021 421 1440/1; map p.136 B1
British Consulate General
8 Riebeeck Street, City Centre; tel: 021 405 2400; map p.136 B2
Canadian High Commission
SA Reserve Bank Building, 60 St George's Mall; tel: 021 423 5240; map p.136 B2
New Zealand Consulate
345 Landsdowne Road, Landsdowne; tel: 021 696 8561
US Consulate General
2 Reddam Avenue, West Lake, Tokai; tel: 021 702 7300

Climate

Cape Town has a Mediterranean climate with four seasons. Winter runs from June to August, when temperatures range from 7–18°C (45–65°F), with pleasant, sunny days scattered between cold, wet ones. From September to November the weather is extremely unpredictable, with anything from hot summer days to a howling southeasterly wind that blows at around 120km/h (75mph). December to March is considered mid summer. The weather is often at its best in March and April, when there is little wind and temperatures are not too stifling. In the interior it becomes very hot in the summer months, and during winter snow falls on the mountain peaks.

In midsummer sunrise is around 5.30am and sundown around 8.30pm. In midwinter it gets dark at about 5.45pm and light at about 7.30am, depending on the cloud cover. There are no time-zone differences within South Africa, and the country has not adopted a daylight-saving system in summer.

Crime and Safety

Since Cape Town is the 2010 Football World Cup host, a lot of effort has been made by government and the police force to tackle the rather worrying problem of crime in the country. Even though South Africa's crime statistics are notoriously high, most of the crime is concentrated in Cape Town's townships, or occurs late at

night in the quieter, darker areas of the city. In the downtown areas closed-circuit TV cameras have been installed on most street corners, keeping an electronic eye on the city, and these have proved to be an effective deterrent.

Be sensible and avoid walking alone after dark in unpopulated streets, and do not draw attention to your money and jewellery.

Gay and Lesbian

If South Africa is the rainbow nation, then the Mother City is the reigning queen. The Cape gay scene is lively and friendly whilst continually making a cultural, political and economic contribution to the city. There are a number of gay-friendly cafés, clubs, steam rooms, restaurants and hotels and designer shops in the City Centre and along the Atlantic Seaboard.
SEE ALSO GAY AND LESBIAN, P.58–9

Health

For a list of registered medical practioners and dentists in your area call **Telkom's Directory Enquiries** (tel: 1023) or the **Talking Yellow Pages** (tel: 10118). The **Cape Town Tourism Bureau** (tel: 021 426 5639) will also gladly assist you.

SAA Netcare Travel Clinic
1107 Picbel Parkade, 58 Strand Street, City Centre; tel: 021 419 3172; www.travelclinic.co.za; Mon–Fri 8am–4pm; map p.136 B2
Caters to the special needs of locals and tourists, offering services like malaria pills, first-aid travel kits and immunisations.

Hospitals

Most hospitals have a 24-hour accident and emergency ward with highly trained doctors.

Christian Barnard Memorial Hospital (tel: 021 480 6111) is situated in the City Centre.

HIV

This destructive disease has been classified as a national pandemic. Due to this, millions of rands are being invested in Aids research and

Left: pay attention to local laws.

Left: The Cape Town Tourism Office at the V&A.

education programmes. For more details contact the **National Aids Helpline** (tel: 0800 012 332; www.aidshelpline.org.za).

Internet

Most hotels, restaurants and cafes have Wi-Fi, although there are still several internet cafés you can find dotted around the busier parts of town. Try **The Info Café** (tel: 021 426 4424) in the City Centre. Many coffee shops such as **Vida e Caffé** now offer Wi-Fi services too.

Money

Most banks are open Mon–Fr 9am–3.30pm, Sat 8am–noon. The unit of currency is the rand (R), divided into 100 cents (c). Notes are issued in R200, R100, R50, R20, R10; coins R5, R2, R1, 50c, 20c, 10c, 5c, 2c. For current currency exchange rates, visit www.xe.com. They are also available at banks and published in the daily press.

Police

If you have been a victim of crime, contact the police at their nationwide number, tel: 10111.

Postal Services

The **South African Post Office** (tel: 0860 111 502; www.sapo.co.za) offers a 24-hour door-to-door service between the major centres in South Africa. Opt for registered mail if sending mail overseas for a safe and timely delivery.

Tipping

A general guideline for tipping in restaurants is between 10 percent and 20 percent of your total bill, porters up to R10 a bag and car guards about R2–R5.

Tourist Information

The **Cape Town Tourism Visitor Centre** (tel: 021 426 4260; www.cape-town.org) is located on the corner of Castle and Burg streets in the CBD. Make it your first port of call if you're unsure what to include in your itinerary, or need maps, tour guides or all the latest information on what's happening in the Mother City. V&A Waterfront also has a smaller visitor centre, the **Cape Town Tourism Office** (tel: 021 405 4500), which is located at the Clock Tower Precinct.

Visa Information

Nationals from the EU, Australia, Canada, the US and Japan do not require a visa for stays less than 90 days. If you require a visa, you must allow at least four weeks to get one before your departure date. Apply for one at your nearest South African Embassy, High Commissioner or Consulate.

> Cape Town is a malaria-free region. However, visitors travelling to certain parts of the country, especially up north, should take necessary precautions. Transmission is at its highest during the warmer and wetter months of November to April when mosquitoes prefer to breed, while the risk is reduced during the drier months from May to October. Visitors to malaria areas should take precautions, bearing in mind that mosquitoes are most prevalent in the evenings.

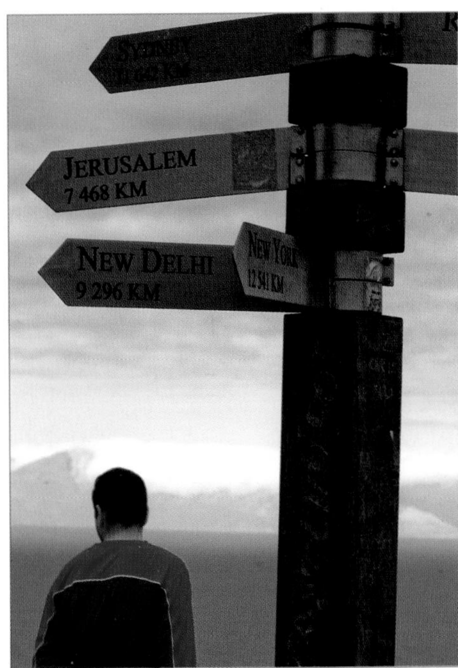

Right: which way is home?

Fashion

Although Capetonians generally appear to be laid-back and casual in their approach, most of them are up-to-the minute on what's hot and what's not to wear. This is a result of many local clothing, shoe and handbag designers being conveniently based in the City Centre and its surrounds. Fashion-savvy travellers will be spoilt for choice when it comes to the variety of different clothing stores to suit their taste. Whether you stumble across secret vintage finds on Long Street or walk the malls for international designer brands, there's something for everyone. For shopping centres, *see also Shopping, p.119.*

Local Designers

Habits

1 Cavendish Close, 1 Cavendish Street, Claremont; tel: 021 671 7330; www.habits.co.za; Mon–Fri 9am–5.30pm, Sat 9am–1.30pm; map p.137 E3

Jenny Le Roux's store is perfect for pick-ups like cashmere jumpers, tailored shirts and fun party frocks for any occasion.

Hip Hop

12 Cavendish Street, Claremont; tel: 021 674 4605; www.hiphopfashion.co.za; Mon–Fri 9am–6pm, Sat 9am–5pm; map p.137 E3

From big voluptuous ball gowns to slinky little cocktail dresses that make a statement, this is the place to find it.

Kluk & Christian Gabriel Du Toit

Portside Centre, Corner of Main and Upper Portswood roads, Green Point; tel: 083 377 7780; www.kluk.co.za; Mon–Fri 9am–6pm; Sat 9am–2pm; map p.133 D3

This design duo are one of the hottest in town, so it's not surprising they have a cult following from around the country. They have a special flair when it comes to flattering the female form, and are especially good for that special little black number.

Lunar

Kildare Centre, 62 Main Street, Newlands; tel: 021 674 6871; Mon–Fri 9am–4.45pm, Sat 9am–2pm

Clean lines, neutral tones and pared-down style is the philosophy behind this classic-contemporary boutique. Book a consultation for the wedding dress of your dreams.

Marion and Lindie

G 231, V&A Waterfront; tel: 021 419 4251; www.marionandlindie.co.za; Mon–Sat 9am–9pm, Sun 10am–9pm; map p.133 E2

Attention to detail, great fabrics and flattering shapes. Cashmere wraps, linen trousers or Grecian gowns – you won't leave empty-handed. The best place to pick up chic maternity wear too.

The Space

Shop L69, Cavendish Square, Claremont; tel: 021 674 6643; www.thespace.co.za; Mon–Sat 9am–7pm, Sun 10am–5pm

Give yourself some time to get through the rails of fabulous hot-off-the-catwalk designs by local designers. Look out for pieces by Amanda Laird Cherry and Colleen Eitzen.

Sun Goddess

Shop 230, Second Level, V&A Waterfront; tel: 021 421 7620; www.sungoddess.co.za; Mon–Sat 9am–9pm, Sun 10am–9pm; map p.133 E2

Husband-and-wife team Thando and Vanya Magaliso have created a unique fashion brand with an African meets global twist.

Left: Cape Town has some great local designers.

safari colours, soft cotton shirts, combat trousers and made-to-fade fabrics in trendy cuts.

Diesel Stylelab
Shop 6277, Victoria Wharf; tel: 021 425 5777; www.diesel.com; daily 9am–9pm; map.133 E2
Cutting-edge, contemporary and deconstructed T-shirts, jeans and dresses. Great underwear too.

Fabiani
Shop 272, Victoria Wharf; tel: 021 425 1810; www.fabiani.co.za; daily 9am–9pm; map p.133 E2
Trademark shirts with the red-cotton last button hole, imported Italian suits and shoes and a good selection of G Star jeans.

Hugo Boss
Shop 6267, Upper Level, Victoria Wharf; tel: 021 421 3052; daily 9am–9pm; map p.133 E2
A brand known for its quality and man-about-town appeal – it would be hard not to treat yourself.

For more shopping opportunities, *see also Food and Drink, p.56–7; Markets, Streets and Squares, p.74–5;* and *Shopping, p.116–19.*

YDE
Shop F60, Cavendish Square, Claremont; tel: 021 683 6177; www.yde.co.za; Mon–Sat 9am–7pm, Sun 10am–5pm
For something young, fresh and funky the Young Designers Emporium is for the dedicated slave to fashion, and reasonably priced too.

Womenswear

Callaghan Collezioni
Shop G46, Ground Floor, Cavendish Square; tel: 021 683 1716; Mon–Sat 9am–7pm, Sun 10am–5pm
Here you'll find the latest imported fashion must-haves from Prada to Diane von Furstenburg and Chloé.

Cigar Clothing
10 Cavendish Street, Claremont; tel: 021 683 3582; www.cigarwomen.co.za; Mon–Sat 8.30am–5.30pm
Ready-to-wear clothes straight from Paris. Great designer jeans and quality linen as well as bags and shoes by local designers.

Lulu Tantan
Shop 7218, 1st Floor, Victoria Wharf; tel: 021 418 8535; daily 9am–9pm; map p.133 E2
Browse through rails of local designers at this Asia-inspired store, or do some damage to your credit card on an antique kimono coat in a bright embroidered silk.

Pure Solid
Shop 6248A, Second level, Victoria Wharf; tel: 021 421 9556; daily 9am–9pm; map p.133 E2
Deconstructed Asian streetwear with focus on A-line dresses, wraparound trousers and blousy patterned cotton shirts.

Left: the Neighbour Goods Market *(see p.74)* also sells clothes.

Menswear

Cape Union Mart
Quay Four, V&A Waterfront; tel: 021 425 4559; www.capeunionmart.co.za; daily 9am–9pm; map p.133 E3
This is the outdoor adventurer's idea of heaven. Mostly

Vintage Clothing

Second Time Around
196 Long Street, City Centre; tel: 021 423 1674; Mon–Fri 9am–5pm, Sat 9am–2pm; map p.136 A2
If you're looking for an old croc clutch bag, knee-length fur coat or sequinned party dress, you won't have to scratch for them at this quaint vintage shop on Long Street.

Stock Exchange
116 Kloof Street, Gardens; tel: 021 424 5971; Mon–Fri 10am–5pm, Sat 10am–1pm; map p.131 E1
A strict policy of only second-hand designer labels from Missoni to Prada, so if the shoe fits, buy it quickly (things fly out of this popular shop).

Film

Cape Town's movie scene is dominated by multiplexes in huge shopping centres, mostly showing mainstream Hollywood feature films. Ster Kinekor is one of the country's principal distributors of movies, along with more arty establishments that one can find at the Victoria and Alfred Waterfront and Cavendish Square in the Southern Suburbs. There's also a handful of independent cinemas set in quirky locations around town that usually host their own interesting line-up of film festivals. Watch the daily press for the latest flicks on show and make a date at the movies.

Local Film

A whole new industry around film has sprung up in the past decade in Cape Town, and there is a continuous stream of Hollywood stars that come to the Mother City for work (and for pleasure). Some locally made feature films are at last receiving recognition. In 2005 *U-Carmen eKhayelitsha* won the Golden Bear for Best Picture in Berlin and *Yesterday* received an Oscar nomination for the Academy's Best Foreign Film. In 2006 the relatively unfancied South African gangster flick *Tsotsi* stole the show at the Academy Awards ceremony, winning the Oscar for the Best Foreign-Language Film. Ironically, the first wave of successful local films had their premières abroad and have hardly ever been screened inside South Africa.

Multiplex Cinemas

Nu Metro

Victoria Wharf, V&A Waterfront; tel: 021 419 9700/ teleticket tel: 086 110 0220; www.numetro.co.za; box offices daily 8.30am–11pm; map p.133 E2

All Nu Metro Cinema complexes in Cape Town show mainstream American films, but you may find a Bollywood hit or controversial documentary on the off chance.

> A ticket to the movies can cost you anything between R25–R40. Children and seniors get lower discounted rates. On Tuesday nights, Ster-Kinekor Movie Club Card holders get in for half-price. For further details and discounts enquire at the ticket-sales office.

Ster-Kinekor Classic

Cavendish Square, 1 Dreyer Street, Claremont; tel: 021 657 5600; www.sterkinekor.com; box offices Mon–Sat 9am–11pm, Sun 11am–9pm

The biggest movie chain in the city, with art-house outlets called Cinema Nouveau. Movie-goers are obliged to use the company's website or ticketline for information and scheduled times.

Independent Cinemas

The Labia

68 Orange Street, Gardens; tel: 021 424 5927; www.labia.co.za; box office daily 11am–8.30pm

This is probably the quirkiest and most nostalgic movie theatre around, with a makeshift bar-meets-café, packets of hot home-made popcorn, and wonderfully oversized wooden armchairs for seating. They show everything from current art-house hits to the odd blockbuster.

Labia on Kloof

Lifestyles on Kloof Centre, 50 Kloof Street, Gardens; tel: 021 424 5927; www.labia.co.za; box office daily 11am–8.30pm; map p.135 E3

Just recently renovated, this is the Labia's smaller sister theatre on trendy Kloof Street, with a liquor licence for those wanting to sip on a nice glass of red before and during the show.

Film Festivals

Suidoosterfees

Jan/Feb; Artscape Theatre, Corner of DF Malan Street and Hertzog Boulevard, Foreshore; tel: 021 421 7839;

Right: The Labia cinema.

Left: *The Choir*, a documentary about a young man in a South African penitentiary, one of many films to première at the TRI Continental Film Festival.

www.artscape.co.za/ www.suidoosterfees.co.za; map p.136 C2
This festival takes it name from the Afrikaans word for the city's prevailing south-easterly wind. It is a multicultural and multilingual event, celebrating numerous art forms in the Western Cape. Its film section is made up of a variety of productions which are either in English or have English subtitles.

Encounters South African International Documentary Festival
July/Aug; Nu Metro, V&A Waterfront; tel: 021 419 9700; www.encounters.co.za; map p.133 E2
Encounters has been going for over a decade and continues to deliver poignant and controversial documentaries to hundreds of Capetonian film-goers. Themes range, but the strong emphasis here is placed on the locally produced films backed up by discussions, research and workshops. Check the website, as the festival may move to later in the year.

TRI Continental Film Festival
Sept; Cinema Nouveau, V&A Waterfront; ticketline: 021 788 5462; www.sterkinekor.com; map p.133 E2
This national film fest showcases relevant and socially aware films about life in Latin America, Asia and Africa.

Out in Africa: South African Gay and Lesbian Film Festival
Nov; Nu Metro, V&A Waterfront; tel: 021 419 9700; www.oia.co.za; map p.133 E2
A long-running gay and lesbian festival featuring short documentaries and films that gets more and more popular each year. This is a not-to-be missed event for those who are tired of the norm.

Food and Drink

A sophisticated food culture has emerged in South Africa. Cape Town is leading the way in terms of rediscovering traditional and regional cuisine and really starting to make its mark on the global food scene. Whether it's the organic and wholefood farmers' markets that are opening up in regenerated industrial areas, or the chic new deli culture focused on beautifully packaged local and seasonal ingredients, you can forget about counting calories whilst travelling around the city and surrounding countryside. For more opportunities to try local produce *see also Markets, Streets and Squares, p.74–5; Restaurants, 102–15.*

Global Influences

Current world food trends are as common in Cape Town as they are anywhere else in the world, but the long list of award-winning chefs and restaurants in the city points to its importance on the food circuit. As much as the city has a window on the world, it still maintains its roots and a deep interest in its own unique style of cuisine. Chefs are adding a new twist to old favourites without compromising the ingredients or nostalgic flavours of the past.

Culinary Traditions

With a rich and diverse cultural heritage there are plenty of culinary traditions for local chefs, cooks and gourmets to draw inspiration from. Whether it's the first Dutch settlers and slaves from Sri Lanka and Indonesia who landed on our shores, to the French Huguenot refugees of the 18th century and the Indian labourers brought to Natal in the 19th century, each has influenced the way South Africans eat and cook today.

African cuisine, mostly slow-cooked and tomato-based, has only in recent years started to emerge as a trend, often reinterpreted and presented in a modern way.

Cape Malay

Cape cuisine is characterised by spiced, curried or sweetened meat, game and fish dishes influenced by East Indian and Asian flavourings and preservatives. The most original dishes are a blend of Dutch and Malay, like *bredies* (slow-cooked stews of meat and vegetables), *sosaties* (skewers of marinated chicken or lamb) and *boboties* (ground minced meat with turmeric and cumin baked with an egg custard topping).

Barbecue

Nothing beats a South African *braai* (barbecue) on a warm summer's day. Alfresco eating and outdoor cooking is a way of life here. *Boerewors* (spicy meat sausage) and lamb chops are a staple on the fire. Other ingredients that usually feature on hot coals include spatch-cocked chicken, T-bone steak or a firm line fish like yellowtail or kingklip stuffed with herbs and lemon quarters that is slowly grilled. Being invited to a *braai* is a very social event, where friends and family gather

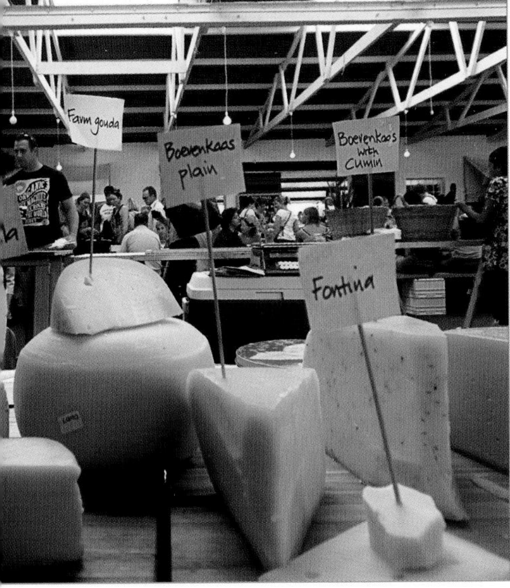

Left: a cheese stall at the Neighbour Goods Market.

Left: *biltong* – dry, cured meat – is a South African speciality.

around the fire, usually with lots of icy cold beer and wine.

Farmhouse Cooking

Much of the country cooking done by the *boere* (farmers) includes dishes like a *potjiekos* (meat or fish stews cooked in a three-legged cast-iron cooking pot on coals), sweet preserves and home-made chutneys, and *biltong* (a snack of wind-dried strips of meat – beef, ostrich or game cured with spices, pepper and herbs). Finish off a typical farmhouse feast with a *melktert* (baked milk custard in a pastry casing) or a *koeksuster* (a moist and syrupy plaited pastry).

Local Ingredients

South Africans are very lucky to live in a land where local produce and ingredients seem to just get better and better. Mediterranean-style cuisines are fitting thanks to the award-winning olives and olive oils produced in the Western Cape. The local cheese-making industry produces a range of classic and more unusual varieties. There are also excellent butchers making a variety of authentic cured meats and sausages, available from most delis. In season, the quality and flavour of fruit, like peaches, grapes, melons and plums you can buy from your local supermarket or street-side vendor, is exceptional.

Cape Town is also one of the best places in South Africa to eat fresh fish and seafood. Enjoy a simply grilled kabeljou, oysters by the dozen, tiger prawns drizzled in lemon butter sauce, and mussels steamed in a white-wine broth.

> You can't go home without tasting South Africa's speciality, **biltong** (dried raw meat), available from various *biltong* kiosks, Pick'n Pay, Woolworths and most butchers. Visitors should know that importing *biltong* into some countries might be illegal.

Game Dishes

Afrikaans country cooking in recent years has made a big comeback, especially with a revival of Louis Leipoldt's recipes and the slow-food movement. Leipoldt was a doctor, writer and gourmet in the 1930s and '40s who collected traditional recipes and developed them into a foundation for a style of Cape cooking. Many of his recipes focused on game meats or venison, which include kudu, springbok, warthog and even giraffe. Simply prepared and slowly cooked over several hours, these meats have an intense flavour enjoyed by keen meat-eaters and the more adventurous diner.

Right: lunch at Mariner's Wharf, Hout Bay.

Markets

Over the last few years there have been a number of markets and farm stalls popping up all over the country, and these have become the place to be and be seen shopping for a Saturday night dinner party.

Neighbour Goods Market
373–375 Albert Road, Woodstock; tel: 021 461 2573; Sat 9am–4pm; map p.137 E3
Held at the Old Biscuit Mill, you'll find everything from bottles of home-made lime cordial to organic meats, cheeses and breads. Have a bite to eat in the central courtyard, like a curry, pizza or wrap and wash it all down with a glass of bubbly or beer. Live music gets everyone into the mood.
SEE ALSO MARKETS, STREETS AND SQUARES, P.74

> There is a long list of local and imported beer to choose from in any restaurant or bar, and it's always served very cold in a chilled glass. Beer is also the drink of choice during any sporting event, especially rugby and cricket.

The Porter Estate Produce Market
Chrysalis Academy, Zwaanswyk Road, Tokai; tel: 082 823 4121; Sat 9am–1pm
Weather dependent, this rustic farmers' market puts on an impressive display of local cheeses, organic vegetables, fresh herbs, preserves and delicious home-baked treats among other things.

Delis

Giovanni's Deliworld
103 Main Road, Green Point; tel: 021 434 6893; Mon–Sun 7.30am–8.30pm; map p.133 C3
Find everything from imported pastas and olive oils to wine, bread and decadent chocolates. On Saturday mornings they sell excellent just-picked organic vegetables, honey and jams from a local farmer.

Melissa's The Food Shop
94 Kloof Street, Tamboerskloof; tel: 021 424-5540; Mon–Fri 7.30am–8pm, Sat–Sun 8am–8pm; map p.135 E4
Beautifully packaged handmade and preservative-free produce. There's also a buffet table where you can enjoy a light and healthy lunch, home-style quiches and cakes. Great biscuits, meringues and jams too.

Cape Wine

The Cape Winelands *(see p.20–1)* are the centre of the Cape wine industry, and in terms of wine production are on a par with some of the better-known wine-producing areas of the world, like Aus-

Right: the Cape Town region produces excellent wine.

Left: refreshments at Neighbour Goods Market.

tralia and France. Right at the heart of the city are the oldest vineyards and those of **Constantia**, whose planting by Huguenot settlers in 1688 predates even those near Bordeaux in France.

Further afield are the country towns of **Stellenbosch** and **Paarl** (rich reds and crisp whites), **Franschhoek** (Semillon and Shiraz) and **Wellington** (whites). Some of the wine estates surrounding these towns, like Meerlust, produce world famous wines. When it comes to varietals, on the red front Shiraz is gaining popularity, while the Pinotage grape is a unique South African cultivar developed from a cross between Pinot Noir and Cinsaut. As for whites, Chenin and Chardonnay dominate the industry.

Buitenverwachting
Klein Constantia Road, Constantia; tel: 021 794 5190; www.buitenverwachting.com; Mon–Fri 9am–5pm, Sat 9am–1pm
Rolling vineyards beneath the Constantiaberg Mountains. Apart from tasting and purchasing wines, visitors can picnic on the lawns under the trees or dine in the restaurant.

Constantia Uitsig
Spaanschemat River Road; tel: 021 794 1810; www.constantia-uitsig.co.za; Mon–Fri 9am–4.30pm, Sat–Sun 10am–4.30pm
A boutique wine estate that has been producing award-winning wines since the 1990s. The terroir is best suited for white wine.

Groot Constantia
Groot Constantia Road, Constantia; tel: 021 794 5128; www.grootconstantia.co.za; May–Oct: 9am–5pm, Nov–Apr: 9am–6pm
Spend a morning or afternoon on the Cape's oldest wine farm sipping on its delicious Sauvignon Blanc, Chardonnay or Gouverneurs Reserve. There's also an adjoining shop selling a range of different wine paraphernalia.

Signal Hill Winery
Mandela Rhodes Place, 23 Church Street, City Centre; tel: 021 422 5206; www.winery.co.za; Mon–Fri 10am–6pm, Sat 10am–2.30pm; map p.136 A2
If you're short of time and can't make it out into the Winelands, don't miss out on this urban winery situated in the new swanky Mandela Rhodes Place development. Here the bulk of the wines are grown on the slopes of Signal Hill in Tamboerskloof, as well as newer vines in Camps Bay and Kalk Bay. Tours and tasting are available six days a week.

> Go on a guided wine route through Stellenbosch, Paarl and Franschhoek and find quality, award-winning wines for as little as R25 a bottle. Or take home some locally produced Rooibos tea, rich in antioxidants and delicious with honey.

Steenberg Vineyards
Corner of Tokai and Steenberg roads, Tokai; tel: 021 713 2211; www.steenberg-vineyards.co.za; Mon–Fri 9am–4.30pm, Sat 10am–2.30pm
An excellent, quaffable Sauvignon Blanc perfect for enjoying over lunches.

WINE BOUTIQUES

Caroline's Fine Wine Cellar
Shop 44, Matador Centre, 62 Strand Street, City Centre; tel: 021 419 8984; www.carolineswine.com; Mon–Fri 9am–5.30pm, Sat 9am–1pm; map p.136 B2
Home to hundreds of top-quality wines with wine-loving staff ready to assist you with the best on offer.

Wine Concepts on Kloof
Shop 15, Lifestyles on Kloof Centre, 50 Kloof Street, Gardens; tel: 021 426 4401; www.wineconcepts.co.za; Mon–Fri 10am–7pm, Sat 9am–5pm; map p.135 E4
The best place to pop into if you need a quick bottle for dinner. Good value, with a range of different varieties to choose from.

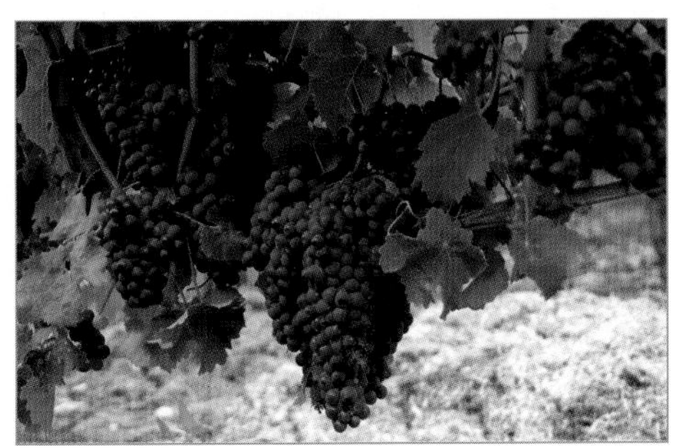

Gay and Lesbian

Cape Town is undoubtedly the gay capital of South Africa. The meeting spot for gay Cape Town has always been De Waterkant Village, a chic suburb next to Green Point which over the years has received a major facelift, and is also home to a number of gay-friendly cafés, clubs, steam rooms, restaurants, hotels and boutique décor and design shops. Travel further along the Atlantic Seaboard and you'll find a colourful array of smaller institutions catering for the gay market. This chapter lists gay-friendly hotels, bars and restaurants, but check the main chapters for further listings.

Accommodation

4 on Varneys
4 Varney Street, Green Point; tel: 021 434 7167; www.4onvarneys.co.za; $$; map p.133 C3
Comfortable rooms with an eclectic mix of furnishings and contemporary artwork. Breathtaking mountain views and home-cooked breakfasts.

Blackheath Lodge
6 Blackheath Road, Sea Point; tel: 021 439 2541; www.blackheathlodge.co.za; $$–$$$
A Victorian oasis complete with swimming pool, stylish suites and very good rates.

Beaches

Sun-worshippers have a choice of white sandy beaches to choose from; the only drawback is the icy-cold temperature of the water. For some social networking spend the day on **Clifton Third Beach**, which is nicely sheltered from the wind, or the secluded **Sandy Bay** nudist beach near Llandudno.
SEE ALSO BEACHES, P.37, 39

Clubs and Bars

The well-known clubbing strip is located on Somerset Road, but over the years the variety of party spots has diminished due to a number of new commercial and property developments being built in the area. But do not be dismayed, a new Pink Block has emerged, with dance clubs and bars that stay open until the early hours of the morning.

Bar Code
18 Cobern Street, off Somerset Road, Green Point; tel: 021 421 5305; www.leatherbar.co.za; Wed–Sat 10pm to late; map p.133 D4
Try to find your way around the maze of dark rooms, hammocks and an outdoor deck area. Spot lots of men sporting interesting leather outfits.

Assistance and information

The Triangle Project (tel: 021 448 3812) provides sexual health education, free walk-in clinics and counselling. The National Aids Helpline (tel: 0800 012 322) provides a confidential, anonymous 24-hour toll-free telephone counselling, information and referral service for those infected and affected by HIV and Aids.

Beulah Bar
Corner of Somerset and Coburn roads, Green Point; tel: 082 565 6174; daily 7pm to late; map p.133 D4
The perfect start to a girls' night out on the town, with two bars and a pumping dance floor playing the latest beats. (Boys and girls.)

Bronx Action Bar
20 Somerset Road, Green Point; tel: 021 419 9216; www.bronx.co.za; daily 8pm to late; map p.133 D4
One of the original gay and lesbian clubs that caters for everyone and anyone. Expect a packed dance floor in the early hours of the morning with some of the hottest tracks around.

The Loft Lounge
24 Napier Street, De Waterkant; tel: 021 425 2647; Tue–Sun 5pm–2am; map p.133 D4
A new kid on the block that's best for pre-clubbing cocktails. A live act sets the scene for a great night ahead.

Restaurants and Cafés

Café Manhattan
74 Waterkant Street, De Waterkant; tel: 021 421 6666;

Left: Bronx Action Bar.

www.manhattan.co.za; daily 9am–1pm; map p.133 D4
This Cape gay institution is best-known for its delicious hamburgers and steaks, and a friendly, relaxed bar area that comes alive after dark. If you're in the mood to meet people, you've come to the right place.

Lazari Food Gallery
Corner of upper Maynard Street and Vredehoek Avenue; tel: 021 461 9865; Mon–Fri 7.30am–5pm, Sat–Sun 8.30am–4pm; map p.136 A4
A stylish and friendly lunching hot spot serving the best eggs Benedict in town. Its wraps, pastas and freshly baked vanilla cupcakes are all brilliant too.

Lola's
228 Long Street, City Centre; tel: 021 423 0885; daily 8am until late; map p.136 A3
A corner café that spills onto the pavement on vibey Long Street. The furniture is 1950s and the clientele quite zany. It serves mostly vegetarian meals and cold beer.

Right: out and about in Cape Town.

Websites
www.lushcapetown.co.za; www.gayromeo.com; www.gaydargirls.com; www.friendsofdorothytours.co.za

On Broadway
88 Shortmarket Street, City Centre; tel: 021 424 1194; www.onbroadway.co.za; daily 6.30pm until late, shows 8.30pm; map p.136 A2
For live entertainment this dinner-show restaurant is your best bet. Check out its website for its show programme, featuring some of the best local musical talent and drag artists.

Parties, Festivals and Events

Cape Town Pride
www.capetownpride.co.za
The Pride Festival brings together a diverse chunk of the Cape Town gay community. The streets of the city come alive Mardi Gras-style with an extravaganza of floats, beautiful bodies and costumes like you've never seen before. The week before the march there's a host of fabulous parties and celebrations not to be missed out on.

The Mother City Queer Project
www.mcqp.co.za
Held every December, this is not to be missed. It's the biggest gathering of gay, lesbian and straight folk and probably the most glamorous party in Africa. The only thing you have to think about is what to wear (each year has a wild theme) and how to strut it on the night. Be prepared for an all-nighter: the music is so good you won't want to go home.

Out in Africa: South African Gay & Lesbian Film Festival
Nu Metro, V&A Waterfront; www.numetro.co.za/ www.oia.co.za
A long-running gay and lesbian film festival showing provocative and funny documentaries and shorts.

The Pink Loerie Festival, Knysna
www.pinkloerie.com
Takes place in Knysna on the Garden Route in the last weekend of April, and is a must. Even though you'll have to drive between four and five hours to get there, the assortment of participants and drag queens (and the beautiful coastal setting) are just a few reasons to make a trip of it.

History

30,000BC
San hunter-gatherers, probably descendants of a Late Stone Age people, live in South Africa area.

AD300
Emergence of Khoikhoi tribes, closely related to the San.

900
Iron Age Bantu-speaking tribes settle in Western Cape.

1487
Portuguese explorer Bartolomew Diaz names the Cape of Good Hope.

1498
Vasco da Gama completes the route to India via the Cape.

1503
Antonio de Saldanha anchors at Table Bay and encounters the Khoisan inhabitants. Francis Drake reaches the Cape.

1647
The Dutch vessel *Haerlem* is wrecked in Table Bay.

1652
Jan van Riebeeck sent to the Cape to establish a supply station.

1658
Slaves arrive from the Dutch East Indies.

1659
The first wine from Cape grapes is pressed.

1679
Simon van der Stel becomes commander of the Cape settlement.

1688
Arrival of 200 French Huguenots.

1713
First smallpox epidemic hits the Khoisan community.

1755
Second smallpox epidemic all but wipes out the Khoisan.

1795–1803
British occupy Cape Town. The colony then reverts to the Dutch.

1814–15
Cape Colony is formally ceded to the British by the Congress of Vienna.

1820
British settlers arrive in Eastern Cape.

1834
Cape slaves are emancipated.

1834–40
The Great Trek.

1854
The Cape establishes its own representative parliament.

1870
Diamonds discovered in Griqualand West; Alfred Dock opens.

1880–1
The first Anglo-Boer War.

1886
Gold is discovered in the Transvaal and the mining town of Johannesburg is founded.

1890
Cecil John Rhodes becomes prime minister of the Cape Colony.

1899–1902
Boers defeated in second Anglo-Boer War.

1910
The Cape becomes legislative capital.

1912
African National Congress (ANC) formed.

1936
Black voters are disenfranchised.

1939
World War II breaks out. South Africa joins the Allies.

1948
New National Party government launches policy of colour segregation.

1950–6
Apartheid entrenched with the Group Areas Act.

1960
Warrants issued to arrest ANC leaders.

1961
The Cape becomes a province of the Republic of South Africa.

1963
ANC leader Nelson Mandela is sentenced to life imprisonment.

1966
60,000 residents of District Six are forcibly removed. Prime Minister Verwoerd is assassinated.

1976
Soweto schoolchildren protest against measures to make Afrikaans an official language in black schools.

1983
The anti-Apartheid United Democratic Front is founded.

1986–9
F. W. de Klerk becomes president.

1990–1
Nelson Mandela released from prison. Apartheid dissolved.

1993
Mandela and F. W. de Klerk jointly receive the Nobel Peace Price.

1994
First democratic general election and a victory for the ANC. Nelson Mandela elected president.

1997
South Africa's new Constitution comes into effect.

1999
Mandela retires. His deputy Thabo Mbeki becomes president following ANC election victory. Robben Island declared a Unesco World Heritage Site.

2004
Third democratic elections. ANC wins a 70 percent majority. South Africa wins the bid to host the football 2010 World Cup.

2005
Mbeki sacks his deputy president, Jacob Zuma, over a corruption scandal.

2006
South Africa legalises same-sex marriage.

2007
Corruption trial of Jacob Zuma continues. South Africa wins the rugby World Cup in France. In December Zuma is elected president of the ANC.

2008
Load-shedding and power outages across the country in a bid to save electricity and carry out maintenance on existing power stations. In September Thabo Mbeki resigns.

Hotels

Cape Town has a wide range of accommodation. A room for the night could be anything you'd expect from a standard chain hotel to an individually decorated Victorian loft with mountain and sea views. Choose from luxury hotels, smaller boutique hotels with all the frills of larger establishments, comfortable bed-and-breakfasts as well as self-catering villa rentals. Whether you're looking for a hip hang-out or a snug home-from-home, you're bound to find accommodation that will suit your needs. Just keep in mind that most hotels fill up pretty quickly over the Christmas summer holidays, so reservations are essential.

City Centre

Daddy Long Legs
134 Long Street; tel: 021 422 3074; www.daddylonglegs.co.za; $; map p.136 A2
A unique, arty boutique backpackers' hotel with a difference. Each of the 13 rooms has been individually decorated by a well-known Cape Town artist. Well priced and central to all the hot spots and tourist attractions in the mother city.

The Grand Daddy
38 Long Street; tel: 021 424 7247; www.daddylonglegs.co.za; $$$; map p.136 B2
Set inside a restored Victorian building, this hip hotel has a good mix of smart yet upbeat interiors with sex appeal. It has a gourmet restaurant with an adjoining bar that's popular over weekends, and it's close to all the action on Long Street.

Price categories are for a double room and are given as a guide only (some include breakfast):
$ under R500
$$ R500–R1,000
$$$ R1,000–R2,000
$$$$ over R2,000

Westin Grand Cape Town
Arabella Quays, 1 Lower Long Street, Convention Square; tel: 021 412 9999; www.westin.com/capetown; $$$$; map p.136 B1
An ultra-cool glass-and-granite structure situated opposite the Cape Town International Convention Centre. There is also a good selection of restaurants and bars to suit your mood, but the rooftop **Arabella Spa** on the 19th floor is where you'll want to spend most of your time overlooking the buzzing city below. This is a popular hotel for bigger groups and corporate types wanting all those state-of-the-art-type mod cons and business facilities.
SEE ALSO PAMPERING, P.94

City Bowl

Cape Cadogan
5 Upper Union Street, Gardens; tel: 021 480 8080; www.capecadogan.co.za; $$; map p.135 E4
Just off Kloof Street, with its selection of restaurants, décor boutiques, cinemas and sidewalk cafés, this hotel has a bohemian edge with

Left: Daddy Long Legs, backpacker haven with a difference.

modern touches. Situated inside a stately two-storey Georgian and Victorian building that has been beautifully restored and decorated, it provides all the home comforts and luxuries that you would expect of a bigger hotel. There's also a new presidential suite, the Owners Villa, for those wanting a little more privacy and space.

Four Rosmead
4 Rosemead Avenue, Oranjezicht; tel: 021 480 3810; www.fourrosmead.com; $$$; map p.139 E1
This boutique guesthouse, built in 1903, has been stylishly renovated to its former glory. Think Cape contemporary-classic interiors with a sophisticated African feel. Upstairs bedrooms have views across the city, Table Mountain and Lion's Head, whilst the rooms downstairs lead onto a quiet landscaped garden. Spend the day lounging around the pool, or enjoy one of many pampering spa treatments that can be arranged.

Note that prices can vary widely within a hotel, and may change according to the time of year. Rooms are often less expensive in the low season or winter months (April–September) so negotiate prices. Published rates are never cast in stone, so it's worth shopping around.

Left: many hotels have excellent bars, *see p.30–5.*

Mount Nelson Hotel
76 Orange Street; tel: 021 483 1000; www.mountnelson.co.za; $$$$; map p.135 E3
Traditionally known as one of the 'Big Five' luxury and most historic hotels in Cape Town. Some illustrious past visitors include Sir Winston Churchill and Lady Colefax. Expect world-class service and out-of-this-world food at the **Cape Colony** restaurant. No surprise it's a favourite amongst international film stars, world leaders and royalty. The recently renovated suites are a fresh modern take on 1950s glamour. Visit the hotel's **Librisa Spa** for some top-class pampering. A regular hot spot amongst locals is the **Planet Champagne Bar** downstairs, noted for its excellent champagne cocktails.
SEE ALSO BARS, P.32; PAMPERING, P.94; RESTAURANTS, P.106

Left: smart but comfortable at The Grand Daddy.

Protea Fire and Ice
Corner of New Church and Bree streets; tel: 021 488 2555; www.proteahotels.com; $$; map p.136 A3
An unexpected hotel with eclectic interiors which combine wacky décor features with high-tech furniture and crystal-dripping chandeliers. Modern and edgy, with minimally furnished rooms and a good bar downstairs for winding down after a long day.

Victoria and Alfred Waterfront

Breakwater Lodge
Portswood Road; tel: 021 406 1911; www.breakwaterlodge.co.za; $$; map p.133 D3
A beautifully restored and converted 19th-century prison building that now offers great-value-for-money accommodation. Whilst the décor and furnishings are fairly basic, the service is good. The modern rooms are

light and breezy (couldn't be less cell-like) with en suite bathrooms and views.

Cape Grace Hotel
West Quay Road; tel: 021 410 7100; www.capegrace.com; $$$$; map p.133 E3
The Cape Grace (a member of the Leading Small Hotels of the World) is the epitome of understated elegance and charm, combining the intimacy of a small hotel with the service and standards of a 'big' hotel. The newly refurbished rooms are well stocked with the usual pampering treats. There's also a wellness spa that incorporates various facets of African traditional healing with beauty treatments. Have a drink downstairs at the **Bascule** whisky bar and wine cellar which stocks a selection of 400 whiskies, followed by a casual meal at **one.waterfront**.
SEE ALSO BARS, P.33; RESTAURANTS; P.107

Radisson SAS Waterfront
Beach Road, Granger Bay; tel: 021 441 3000; www.radissonsas.com; $$$; map p.133 D2
An ideally situated hotel within walking distance of the V&A Waterfront, perched on the water's edge at Granger Bay. Suites are comfortable and modern with all the necessary amenities, including use of the **Onewellness Spa**. Sip a gin and tonic in the rimflow pool downstairs as you watch an electric orange and pink sunset over the ocean.
SEE ALSO PAMPERING, P.94

The Table Bay
Quay 6; tel: 021 406 5000; www.suninternational.com; $$$$; map p.133 E2
A popular hotel for bigger tour groups, this established waterfront hotel is well situated for those wanting to be in close proximity to shops, yachts and tourist attractions. There is a fully equipped state-of-the-art gymnasium and the excellent **Camelot Spa**.
SEE ALSO PAMPERING, P.94

Southern Suburbs

Banksia Boutique Hotel
14 Banksia Road, Rosebank; tel: 021 689 2992; www.banksiaboutique.co.za; $$
A Victorian home of enormous

Right: the elegant Cape Grace Hotel.

Left: The Table Bay is situated right on the waterfront.

proportions. Only 15 minutes from the city, this enchanting boutique hotel has everything you could possible need, including a 12-metre (395ft) indoor swimming pool. Bedrooms are plushly decorated with soft throws and contemporary classic furniture.

The Vineyard Hotel and Spa

Colinton Road, Newlands; tel: 021 657 4500; www.vineyard.co.za; $$$

A recent expansion to this large hotel now includes the spacious 'Riverside De Luxe Suites', which feature a modern, Zen style of décor. Other rooms are arranged around a Japanese-style courtyard, and Mountain rooms are named for their lovely views. Interiors are chic and modern with generous bathrooms, natural stone tiles, muted fabrics and mahogany wood furnishings. Wall-length sliding doors front each ground-floor unit, with a sunny outdoor terrace. Enjoy an authentic Thai massage available at the world-class **Angsana Spa** right next door.

SEE ALSO PAMPERING, P.94

Constantia Valley

The Constantia

Spaanschemat River Road, Constantia; tel: 021 794 6561; www.theconstantia.com $$$

Spacious, well-appointed rooms in the heart of the Constantia winelands. Country-style accommodation and a full English breakfast that is so good, it will keep you going all day long.

Constantia Uitsig Hotel and Spa

Constantia Uitsig; tel: 021 794 6500; www.constantia-uitsig.com; $$$

Apart from the award-winning **La Colombe** restaurant and its excellent wines, the Constantia Uitsig Hotel and spa consists of 16 luxury garden rooms charmingly decorated in a country style with sunny balconies and a pool where guests can relax. If it's peace and quiet you're after, this is where it's at.

SEE ALSO RESTAURANTS, P.109

Steenberg Hotel and Winery

Steenberg Estate, Tokai Road, Constantia; tel: 021 713 2222; www.steenberghotel.com; $$$$

As one of the oldest wine farms in the Constantia Valley, with its historical buildings still intact, owner and entrepreneur Graham Beck

Price categories are for a double room and are given as a guide only (some include breakfast):
$ under R500
$$ R500–R1,000
$$$ R100–R2,000
$$$$ over R2,000

is breathing new life into this luxurious five-star hotel and winery. The newly opened Heritage suites are enormous (160sq metres/191sq yds) with private pools and a casual, bistro-style eatery, **Catharina's**, inside the old cellar.

SEE ALSO RESTAURANTS, P.108

Atlantic Seaboard and Cape Peninsula

The Bay Hotel

69 Victoria Road, Camps Bay; tel: 021 430 4444; www.thebayhotel.co.za; $$$$; map p.138 A4

This Miami-style hotel located on Cape Town's prime strip of beachfront in Camps Bay is everything cool, crisp and minimalist. Some of the amenities guests can enjoy include a hair salon, boutique shops and a good restaurant (even though you will be spoilt for choice when it comes to eateries in the area). The alfresco beach

bar, **Sandy B**, is great for sundowners on a hot summer's evening overlooking the rim flow pool and turquoise bay.

Hout Bay Manor
Main Road, Hout Bay; tel: 021 790 0116; www.houtbaymanor.co.za; $$$
Built in 1871, this hotel is a national monument that recently underwent a major refurbishment. It now has a more contemporary African feel that's exploding with bright colours and interesting knick-knacks. Hout Bay Manor offers affordable luxury with all the mod cons, a gourmet restaurant, **Pure**, and all the luxury goodies you could possibly want during your stay, like complimentary beach towels, hats and nibbly treats to eat all day long.

Sugar Hotel
1 Green Point Main Road; tel: 021 439 3780; www.sugarhotel.co.za; $$; map p.133 D4
An intimate boutique hotel where chic travelling urbanites overnight partly because of the excellent business facilities and the proximity to the city's hot spots. All the rooms are contemporary in style, with flatscreen TVs and DVD players. There's also a vibey bar, restaurant and beauty spa where guests meet and mingle.

Twelve Apostles Hotel and Spa
Victoria Road, Oudekraal, Camps Bay; tel: 021 437 9000; www.12apostleshotel.com; $$$$; map p.133 A3
Set between mountain and sea on the Atlantic coast, this laid-back five-star hotel is a true getaway for those who don't want to be based in the city itself. It has a variety of chic sea-view and mountain-

Right: the Cape Dutch D'Ouwe Werf.

Left: the Twelve Apostles Hotel and Spa.

facing rooms. The adjoining **Sanctuary Spa** offers indulgent body-and-health treatments inside a cave-like space (previously an old cellar), with flotation tanks and steam rooms. South African food is served at the **Azure** restaurant, overlooking the ocean, or at the more informal deli upstairs in a fynbos garden.
SEE ALSO PAMPERING, P.95

The Village Lodge
49 Napier Street, De Waterkant; tel: 021 421 1106; www.thevillagelodge.co.za; $$$; map p.133 D4
A 15-bedroom boutique hotel, a private villa and several fully furnished self-catering townhouses in this trendy and centrally located area. The rooftop pool at the main lodge is a highlight, should you want to arrange a private drinks party with spectacular views of Table Mountain.

Cape Winelands

Akademie Street Guesthouses
Akademie Street, Franschhoek; tel: 021 876 3027; www.aka.co.za; $$
Each of the three five-star guesthouses has its own personality and charm. The double-storey Gelatenheid has a loft with a big balcony and a secret Victorian bath under the trees. Oortuiging is situated under the shade of a gigantic stinkwood tree with its own private garden and pool. Vreugde also opens onto a quiet garden with French doors. The perfect retreat for a romantic weekend away.

D'Ouwe Werf
30 Church Street, Stellenbosch; tel: 021-887 4608; www.ouwewerf.com; $$$
Established in the heart of Old Stellenbosch in 1802, this plush inn is a real gem – notable for its authentic Cape Dutch architecture, period décor, personal service, sumptuous traditional Cape cuisine and quality wine list.

Klein Genot Wine and Country Estate
3 Green Valley Road, Franschhoek; tel: 021 876 2738; www.kleingenot.co.za; $$
A country getaway complete with a spa, rolling meadow gardens and six comfortably decorated en suite rooms with their own fireplaces and little nooks where you can laze in the afternoon sun. Enjoy a full organic farm-style breakfast that will leave you wanting to come back again for more.

Price categories are for a double room and are given as a guide only (some include breakfast):
$ under R500
$$ R500 – R1000
$$$ R1000 –R2000
$$$$ over R2000

La Résidence
Elandskloof Private Road, Franschhoek; tel: 021 876 4100; www.laresidence.co.za; $$$$
This is without a doubt the most glamorous country boutique hotel to open in the Cape's gourmet capital of Franschhoek. Situated on a 30-acre (12-hectare) estate of vineyards, orchards and established oaks, this private luxury hideaway in the heart of wine country consists of 11 elegant suites, each with

its own statement-making personality. Beds are layered in pure linen, fabrics are sumptuous, and the one-off furniture pieces and rugs add an oriental touch. Food is top-notch and prepared by the talented in-house chef.

Lanzerac Hotel and Spa
Lanzerac Street, Jonkershoek Road, Stellenbosch; tel: 021 887 1132; www.lanzerac.co.za; $$$$
This 300-year-old manor house is set amongst award-winning vineyards, beautifully landscaped gardens and centuries-old oak trees. Five-star suites, Cape Malay cuisine and a recently opened wellness centre and spa.

Le Quartier Francais
16 Huguenot Road, Franschhoek; tel: 021 876 2151; www.lequartier.co.za; $$$$
A small but exceptional guest-house in the heart of the Winelands' most scenic village. Its focus is an award-winning restaurant, **The Tasting Room**, under the helm of chef Margot Janse.
SEE ALSO RESTAURANTS, P.113

Mont Rochelle Hotel and Mountain Vineyards
Dassenberg Road, Franschhoek; tel: 021 876 2770; www.montrochelle.co.za; $$$$
Expect luxury and seclusion at this gourmet destination set amongst 40 acres (16 hectares) of mountain vineyards. The hotel's all-new 16 ensuite bedrooms and six suites are spread out over three wings of the hotel, creating that feeling of staying in a sprawling country house rather than a large impersonal hotel. Dinner at **Mange Tout** restaurant is a gastronomic affair, whilst wine-tastings take place in the old fruit packing shed, recently restored and transformed into a boutique cellar.

Overberg

Arniston Hotel
Arniston; tel: 028 445 9000; www.arnistonhotel.com; $
The best hotel in the region, with a great location directly opposite the turquoise-tinted ocean. Recently refurbished, all the rooms are rather basic yet comfortable (pool-facing rooms are less windy), and the freshly prepared line fish of the day is almost always excellent. G&Ts on the terrace overlooking the ocean is a must-do.

Marine Hermanus
Marine Drive, Hermanus; tel: 028-313 1000; www.collectionmcgrath.com; $$$$
Situated on the craggy cliffs close to the town centre and Old Harbour, this is the grande dame of Hermanus (built in 1902). Rooms are all tastefully decorated with views across Walker Bay or the Kleinriviersmond Mountains. This Relais & Châteaux establishment also offers a choice of two fine restaurants, including the excellent **Seafood at the Marine**, along with a new sun terrace and the Seafood

> For a truly African experience, try spending at least one night at a township bed-and-breakfast in Langa or Khayelitsha where you will enjoy warm and honest lodging with welcoming hosts. For details contact Sivuyile Tourism Centre, tel: 021 637 8449.

Right: the grandly situated Plettenberg hotel.

Left: Marine Hermanus.

Express Café, which serves up great sashimi.
SEE ALSO RESTAURANTS, P.114

Garden Route

Acorn Guest House
4 Kerk Street, George; tel: 044 874 0474; www.acornguest house.co.za; $$
A renovated Victorian house conveniently situated near the best restaurants and sights of George, with comfortable bedrooms, pool deck and wireless internet.

The Grand
Main Road, Plettenberg Bay; tel: 044 533 3301; www.the grand.co.za; $$$$
Stylish, quirky and classy, the Grand is one of the most interesting destinations in Plettenberg Bay. It's all about easy, bohemian living with witty elements at every turn. The spacious and sumptuous bedrooms have shuttered doors leading onto balconies with views across the bay. Spend your days lounging around the pool on comfy, cushioned daybeds.

Knysna Quays Protea
51 Main Street, Knysna; tel: 044 382 2127; www.proteahotels.com; $$$
A simple yet quality hotel, with air conditioning, telephone in rooms, facilities for disabled guests and a gleaming swimming pool. Situated close to the harbour, boutique décor and curio shops and the lagoon.

Price categories are for a double room and are given as a guide only (some include breakfast):
$ under R500
$$ R500–R1,000
$$$ R1,000–R2,000
$$$$ over R2,000

The Plettenberg
40 Church Street, Plettenberg Bay; tel: 044 533 2030; www.collectionmcgrath.com; $$$$
A grand hotel in English country-house style, with good food and sea views. There is an alfresco outdoor terrace and pool overlooking the bay, where you may get lucky and spot a whale or two.

Protea Hotel Old Post Office Square
Bartolomeu Dias Museum Complex, Mossel Bay; tel: 044 691 3738; www.oldposttree.co.za; $
Built as a warehouse in 1846, this historic hotel has an attractive waterfront location in the town centre and 30 smart rooms with modern amenities.

Language

South Africa is not called the Rainbow Nation for nothing – especially considering it's a multilingual country with 11 official languages and many others – African, European, Asian and more – all spoken here at the crossroads of Southern Africa. The country's Constitution guarantees equal status to all these recognised languages in order to cater for the country's diverse population and cultures. English is generally understood across the country, being the language most used in business, politics and the media. However, it only ranks fifth out of the 11 as a home language.

Languages of South Africa

Languages widely spoken today include: **Afrikaans**, **English**, **IsiNdebele**, **IsiXhosa**, **IsiZulu**, **Sepedi**, **Sesotho**, **Setswana**, **SiSwati**, **Tshivenda** and **Xitsonga**. Other languages spoken in South Africa and mentioned in the Constitution are the **Khoi**, **Nama** and **San** languages, sign language, **Arabic**, **German**, **Greek**, **Gujarati**, **Hebrew**, **Hindi**, **Portuguese**, **Sanskrit**, **Tamil**, **Telegu** and **Urdu**.

There are also a few indigenous creoles and pidgins. IsiZulu, IsiXhosa, SiSwati and IsiNdebele are collectively referred to as the **Nguni** languages, as they all have similarities in syntax and grammar. The **Sotho** languages like Setswana, Sepedi and Sesotho also have a lot in common.

> Brush up on your Mother City lingo with these few words: *Bakkie* – a light goods vehicle; *Bergie* – a homeless person; *Braai* – a South African barbecue; *Robot* – a traffic light; *Shebeen* – a township bar.

AFRIKAANS

Afrikaans has its roots in 17th-century Dutch, with different influences from English, Malay, German, Portuguese, French and some parts of African languages. Initially known as Cape Dutch, Afrikaans was largely spoken by people living in the Cape at the time, with Dutch as a more formal way of communicating. As the Afrikaner identity grew, so did the language. In 1925 it was declared an official language (with English) and later in 1948 it played a role in the forming of Afrikaner nationalism and Apartheid. Today it is predominantly spoken by white Afrikaners, 'coloured' South Africans and in a small part of the black population.

Afrikaans Language Museum
Gideon Malherbe House, 11 Pastorie Avenue; tel: 021 872 3441; www.taalmuseum.co.za; Mon–Fri 9am–5pm; entrance charge

If travelling through the Paarl Winelands, take a quick break at the Afrikaans Language Museum, with its insights into the Afrikaner language and culture. Understand its evolution from Dutch and Arabic to 'Kitchen Dutch' to its 'alternative' Afrikaner present as understood today.

ENGLISH

Today English is the country's lingua franca and a compulsory subject in all schools, and the medium of instruction in most senior and tertiary institutions. As a home language, English is spoken by 10 per-

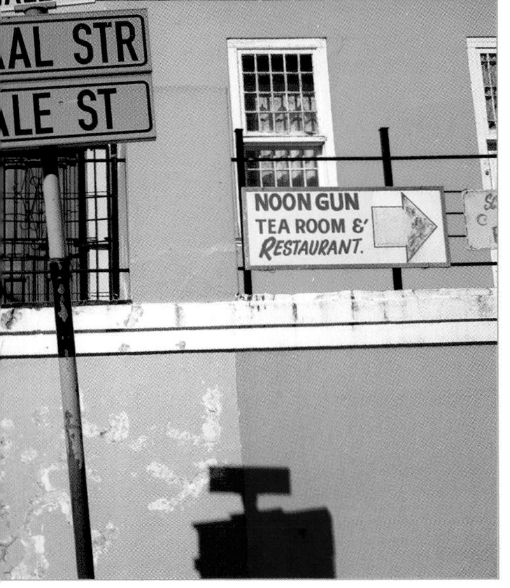

Left: street names in Bo-Kaap.

Tsotsi taal is an amalgam of Afrikaans, English and a number of African languages widely spoken in urban areas by men. The word *tsotsi* means 'gangster', while *taal* is Afrikaans for 'language'. **Fanagalo** is a pidgin that started many years ago in the gold mines up north as a communication between white supervisors and African labourers during the colonial and Apartheid eras. It is essentially a simplified version of IsiZulu and IsiXhosa and tends to follow an English word order.

cent of the population – one in three of which are not white.

ISINDEBELE
Originally an offshoot of the Nguni people of KwaZulu-Natal. Today it is a tonal language mainly spoken in the provinces of Limpopo, Mpumalanga and Gauteng.

ISIXHOSA
South Africa's second-largest language-closely related to IsiZulu and mainly spoken in the former Transkei, Ciskei and Eastern Cape areas. Some famous Xhosa include Nelson Mandela and former president Thabo Mbeki.

ISIZULU
This is the language of the largest ethnic groups, the Zulu people who take their name from the chief who founded the royal line in the 16th century. Probably the most widely understood language spoken in Cape Town, Gauteng and even Zimbabwe, but mainly concentrated in KwaZulu-Natal.

SEPEDI
Otherwise known as northern sotho or Sesotho, Sepedi is mostly spoken in the province of Limpopo up north.

SESOTHO
This is the language of Lesotho, a country entirely surrounded by South African territory as well as the Free State and south of Gauteng. This is one of the first African languages to be used in the written form.

SETSWANA
This is the language of the Tswana people in Botswana but also spoken in the Northern Cape regions. A famous Setswana-speaker was the intellectual journalist and writer Sol T. Plaatje – one of the founder members of the African National Congress.

SISWATI
You'll hear this language in the country of Swaziland and in eastern Mpumalanga – also closely related to IsiZulu.

TSHIVENDA
An isolated language spoken only by the Venda people who are culturally closer to the Shona people of Zimbabwe.

XITSONGA
The Tsonga people first settled in the Limpopo River Valley, but spread through the eastern Limpopo and Mpumalanga into the borders of Mozambique.

Right: Afrikaans is widely used by white Capetonians.

Literature

Written literature does not exist in all of South Africa's 11 official languages; most of it is found in English, with a very strong, especially poetic, tradition in Afrikaans. This section introduces some of the local South African writers who have put the country on the literary map as well as a listing of books and bookshops around town where you can browse or buy some of their well-known works. Some of the better-known bookshops have adjoining cafés where you can spend a few hours paging though your new book with a great-tasting coffee and slice of cake on the side.

Local Literary Culture

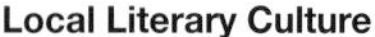

The end of Apartheid and the emergence of a democratic South Africa in 1994 created an entirely new social environment based on a constitution that promises freedom of speech and expression. It was at this time that many famous black writers, such as **Zakes Mda**, returned from exile, and the luminary **Wally Serote** advised the president on literature and heritage. **J.M.Coetzee** wrote most of his works in Cape Town and in 2004 was awarded the Nobel Prize in Literature, an honour previously given to another South African author, **Nadine Gordimer** in 1991. One of the best-known Cape Town writers is best-selling author **Wilbur Smith**. The best-selling Afrikaans writer **André Brink** lives in Cape Town, and most of his works have been translated into every major language. Most of these writers wrote their books through the struggle years of Apartheid and continue to play an imperative role in the shaping of a literary culture for the future.

Bookshops

A is for Apple

16B Kloof Nek Road, Tamboerskloof; tel: 021 424 5409; www.aisforapple.co.za; Mon–Fri 9am–5.30pm, Sat 9am–2.30pm; map p.135 D4

A pretty little bookshop that specialises in books for children. There is a kiddies' coffee bar serving biscuits and decaf coffee. They also have 'story hours' held weekly in the reading nook, which is perfect for any parent looking for some time out.

Biblioteq

41 Kloof Street, City Bowl; tel: 021 422 0774; Mon–Fri 10am–5.30pm, Sat 10am–3pm; map p.135 E4

An art gallery-meets bookstore in a slick space offering a selection of mainly limited edition books on art, design and visual culture. Visitors can also expect a variety of unexpected finds by some of the world's leading pop artists or classic cult photographers.

Clarke's Bookshop

211 Long Street, City Centre; tel: 021 423 5739; www.clarkesbooks.co.za; Mon–Fri 9am–5pm, Sat 9am–1pm; map p.136 A2

A purveyor of new, second-hand and out-of-print books on Cape Town and South Africa. Probably the best source for political musings on South Africa and the world. A good place to find local novelists. Well worth a browse.

Exclusive Books

Shop 6160, Victoria Wharf, V&A Waterfront; tel: 021 419 0905; www.exclusivebooks.com; Mon–Thur 9am–10.30pm, Fri–Sat 9am–11pm, Sun

Left: a cosy neighbourhood bookstore.

Even though South Africa has many desperate needs in terms of crime and poverty, the new democratic government is far more enlightened about art and literature than the old Apartheid regime and has grasped the important role that culture plays in education and reconciliation.

9am–9pm; map p.133 E2
This is South Africa's national chain (there are five more in Cape Town). Spend the afternoon reading a book or the latest glossy magazine from around the world in the store's coffee shop. It stocks design and coffee-table books galore and some international papers hot off the press. Also has a range of smart notebooks and journals on offer, as well as luxury sheets of giftwrap and an assortment of greeting cards.

Quagga Art and Books
84 Main Road, Kalk Bay; tel: 021 788 2752; Mon–Sat 9.30am–5pm, Sun 10am–5pm
An interesting collection of art, artefacts and dusty first-edition books. An excellent range of Africana, including some old maps, photographs and books. Lots of second-hand books too. They also sell some interesting antiquarian objects for your home library.

Left: The Traveller's Bookshop at Victoria Wharf.

The Traveller's Bookshop
Shop 2, King's Warehouse, Victoria Wharf, V&A Waterfront; tel: 021 425 6880, Mon–Sat 9am–10pm, Sun 10am–9.30pm; map p.133 E2
The globe-trotter's bookshop for all the guides, coffee-table books or fold-up maps you may need for a trip, or just for interest's sake. A comprehensive choice of specialist armchair travel, and all the information you may need about South Africa from its cities to its surrounding neighbours.

Wordsworth Books
Shop 7103 Victoria Wharf, V&A Waterfront; tel: 021 425 6880; Mon–Sat 9am–10pm, Sun 10am–9.30pm; map p.133 E2
This is one of several Wordsworth shops in Cape Town, where friendly, well-read staff are happy to give you a review of the latest best-sellers or perhaps a discount for bulk purchasing. It stocks everything from thrillers to arty guidebooks and local best-sellers.

Further Reading List

CULTURE

Magnificent South Africa by Elaine Hurford and Peter Joyce. A visual journey through South Africa covering geography, history and the people.

FICTION

The Conservationist by Nadine Gordimer. A 1974 Booker Prize-winner by this highly acclaimed South African writer.

Disgrace by J.M Coetzee. A cynical look at South African society which won the 1999 Booker Prize.

HISTORY AND BIOGRAPHY

Long Walk to Freedom by Nelson Mandela. A compelling must-have autobiography for anyone coming to South Africa.

Tomorrow is Another Country by Allister Sparks. Follows the transition from Apartheid to democracy.

A History of South Africa by Frank Welsh. A comprehensive and readable history from colonial times to a rainbow nation.

NATURE AND HIKING

Best Walks in the Cape Peninsula by Mike Lundy. Features some of the best viewpoints, caves and walks.

Mammals of Southern Africa by Charles and Tilde Stuart. A useful guide for those who are going into the wilderness.

Markets, Streets and Squares

Taking a leisurely stroll around Cape Town, you are guaranteed to stumble across many lively open-air markets and pedestrianised malls and squares that come alive during the day with arts and crafts traders, food vendors, artists, noisy gumboot dancers and buskers performing on the pavements. They're also the best places to find alfresco restaurants and cafés for a leisurely bite to eat and a chance to do some people-watching. For details of where to find more fresh produce, *see also Food and Drink, p.56–7.*

Left: mushrooms at the Neighbour Goods Market.

Markets

Church Street Antique Market

Church Street, City Centre; Mon–Sat 9am–4pm; map p.136 A2

This is a very informal antique market, where antique specialists set up their wares on long trestle tables. Find everything from vintage clothing to silver crockery, books and costume jewellery. There are also a number of other interesting Africana shops, bookstores and cafés.

Milnerton Flea Market

Racecourse Road, Milnerton; Sat–Sun 7am–5pm

This is a weekend boot sale that has become a hot spot for bargain-hunters. Find everything from old kitchenalia to costume jewellery and furniture. Eat some of the pancakes sprinkled with sugar and cinnamon for a mid-morning treat. An all-round eye-opening experience.

> At the Pan-African Market there are three storeys of rooms which overflow with goods from all over Africa, from tin picture frames to large, intricate carvings and delicate beadwork. There's also a small café serving traditional African cuisine on the first-floor balcony.

Neighbour Goods Market

The Old Biscuit Mill, 373–375 Albert Road, Woodstock; tel: 021 462 6361; shops: Mon–Fri 9am–4.30pm, Sat 9am–2pm, farmers' market: Sat 9am–4pm; map p.137 E3

An extremely popular Saturday-morning market in the renovated Pyotts Biscuit Mill. This is where the hip and happening hang out every Saturday morning and shop for delicious local nosh. At the neighbouring shops you will find décor pieces, ceramic art, beads and ironwork, as well as clothing by local emerging designers. Get there early or miss out on the action.

SEE ALSO FOOD AND DRINK, P.56

Pan-African Market

76 Long Street, City Centre; tel: 021 426 4478; www.panafrican.co.za; Mon–Fri 8.30am–5.30pm, Sat 8.30am–3.30pm; map p.136 B1

A beautifully preserved building where you'll find over 30 stalls representing over 14 African countries offering a vast range of different craft, cuisine and clothing. A vibrant shopping experience.

Rondebosch Village Market

St Andrews Road, Rondebosch; tel: 021 696 5749; Sat mornings

Lovers of organic fruit, freshly baked breads and artisan cheeses head to this market early on a Saturday morning to fill up their shopping baskets. There's also a small selection of woodware and plants.

Left: the Neighbour Goods Market.

a touch-screen directory at the top of the mall, and policeman monitor the area, some on horseback, to keep an eye on pickpockets.

> Tourist attractions like popular flea markets and squares that are very busy during the day are also filled with pickpockets and muggers, so try to avoid carrying any valuables around with you. Be alert at all times.

Streets

Long Street Antique Arcade

127 Long Street, City Centre; tel: 021 423 3585; Mon–Fri 9am–4.30pm, Sat 9am–2pm; map p.136 A2

This is a great spot to spend a few hours browsing the quaint stores for interesting collectables. Some are specialists in china and hallmarked silverware, while others stock twinkly Victorian and Edwardian jewellery.

Mandela Rhodes Place

Corner of Church Street and St Georges Mall, City Centre; map p.136 A2

An exciting new development housing a handful of gourmet restaurants, boutique shops, a wine bar and an urban winery. This is also a smart new address with high-tech facilities and 24-hour security for those looking to live in the centre of town.

St Georges Mall

St Georges Street, City Centre; map p.136 B2

This is a charming cobblestone pedestrian street filled with midday lunching spots, street vendors, artists, banks (with foreign exchange), statues, sculpture, big department stores and buskers. This open-air mall starts at St Georges Cathedral in Adderley Street and extends all the way to the foreshore. There is

Squares

Greenmarket Square

Corner of Shortmarket and Berg streets, City Centre; Mon–Fri 10am–5pm, Sat 10am–4pm; map p.136 B2

A must-visit for all first-timers to the Mother City. In the past this is where farmers brought their fruit and vegetables to earn some cash. Today this is where vendors, mostly immigrants from all over Africa, gather and sell their crafts and wares. A smattering of clothing stores too. The stately Old Townhouse also looks onto the square.

Heritage Square

Corner of Bree and Shortmarket streets, City Centre; www.heritage.org.za; map p.136 A2

A recently renovated block of 18th-century Georgian and Dutch townhouses. Today it houses a hotel and a handful of restaurants, and the buzzing wine bar **Caveau**. Sit in the courtyard area and watch one of the country's oldest grapevines in action.
SEE ALSO BARS, P.32

Right: crafts at the Pan-African Market on Long Street.

Museums and Galleries

Take a stroll down Cape Town's 'Museum Mile' and discover a host of different museums, each with an interesting story to tell of the city's past. Many national monuments and heritage sites house some of the most noteworthy period art, artefacts and furniture found in the country. If you're looking to hit the classic or contemporary art scene, Cape Town has it all. Today not only are more attractions open to the public, but they also display a sense that the city's cultural patrimony at last belongs to everyone.

Museums

CITY CENTRE AND CITY BOWL

Bertram House

Hiddingh Campus, Orange Street, Gardens; tel: 021 424 9381; www.iziko.org.za/bertram; view by appointment; entrance charge; map p.136 A3

A small, little-known museum housing the Winifred Ann Lidderdale Bequest – a collection of English porcelain, silver and 19th-century furniture. The late-Georgian, red-brick building stands at the top of the Avenue, shaded by the oaks on the university's Hiddingh Hall campus and facing the magnificent columned entrance to the sumptuous Mount Nelson Hotel *(see p.63)*.

Castle of Good Hope

Military Museum, Corner of Buitenkant and Darling streets, City Centre; tel: 021 787 1249; www.castleofgoodhope.co.za; daily 9am–4pm; entrance charge; map p.136 B3

Visitors enter the castle through a handsome gate, topped by a 17th-century bell tower, on the castle's north-west side. Commissioner Van Rheede van Oudtshoorn was responsible for building the Kat, a 12-metre (40ft) high building slicing across the open courtyard. Most famously it houses the bulk of the William Fehr Collection of Africana – oil paintings, furniture, silverware, glass, carpets and porcelain relating to the Cape's earliest colonial period. Diagonally opposite

> Slaves born in the Slave Lodge at the time were baptised and could not be sold to private individuals. They also received an education (in Dutch) up to the age of 12. They were taught by fellow slaves or freed slaves, who received a salary.

Left: Iziko South African National Gallery *(see p.84)*.

Left: relics of Cape Town's past at the District Six Museum.

the Kat wall, between the Catzenellenbogen and Burren towers, is the **Military Museum**, which gives you a peek in to the Cape's defence history. Artefacts on display include an enormous wooden horse (1898) employed by the Cape Field Artillery to introduce recruits to the secrets of harnessing and saddling, as well as a collection of beautifully crafted 18th-century swords, regimental costumes and documents on colonial expansion. There is a particularly interesting section on the Boer War.

SEE ALSO ARCHITECTURE, P.28

District Six Museum

25A Buitenkant Street, City Centre; tel: 021 466 7200; www.districtsix.co.za; Mon 9am–2.30pm, Tue–Sat 9am–4pm; entrance charge; map p.136 B3

District Six was originally a lively, colourful neighbourhood populated by the descendants of freed slaves, artisans, tailors, merchants, labourers and immigrants. It was a relatively poor area, but its inhabitants had lived there for many generations. In 1966, under the Group Areas Act it was declared a White Group Area, and for the next 15 years a policy of systematic forced removal of the inhabitants and the destruction of their homes and workshops was pursued until there was virtually nothing left.

The museum commemorates the community and illustrates the resulting devastation of the lives and livelihoods of its inhabitants. There are maps, photographs and poignant reminders of a neighbourhood sadly gone. A room in a typical home of the neighbourhood has been recreated, along with a school house, a barber's shop and other original settings, all enlivened with evocative recordings of District Six inhabitants relating their stories. It offers a guided tour of the area by an ex-resident, but these tours must be booked well in advance

Gold of Africa Museum

96 Strand Street, Martin Melck House, City Centre; tel: 021 405 1540; www.goldofafrica.com; Mon–Sat 9.30am–5pm; entrance charge; map p.136 A1

This is the city's newest museum and well worth a visit. Established by AngloGold, the world's largest gold-mining company, it houses a stunning collection of gold-jewellery and cultural artefacts from around the African continent. There are examples from Mali, Senegal and Ghana – but there are items from Zimbabwe and South Africa as well, from ceremonial objects used by royalty to smaller amulets carried by traders and warriors. Pieces are

Right: gold sandals from the Gold of Africa Museum.

beautifully displayed, with good background information on the cultural and symbolic importance of gold in African cultures. The museum is housed in the Martin Melck House, a fine original townhouse dating from 1788. There is a delightful courtyard café that serves coffee and cakes, an excellent selection of wine and light meals.

Iziko Slave Lodge Museum

49 Adderley Street; tel: 021 460 8242; www.iziko.org.za/slavelodge; Mon–Sat 10am–5pm; entrance charge, free Sat; audio tours available; map p.136 B2

Built in 1679, after the Castle of Good Hope this is the second-oldest colonial building in Cape Town. It began life as a shelter for slaves of the Dutch East India Company, brought to Cape Town from India, Madagascar, Ceylon (Sri Lanka), Malaya (British-controlled Malaysia) and Indonesia. Following the abolition of slavery in 1834 the building became the city's first post office, then the library and then the supreme court.

The museum's new focus on the building's history as a slave lodge is fascinating. An audio tour explains the original purpose of each room and describes the horrifying lives endured by the slaves. Inspect the latrines in the courtyard, the hospital, dungeons and executioner's room. The lodge once held an average of 500 slaves, rising to 1,000 at its peak. Today it has been beautifully restored, and is a pleasant lunch-hour retreat for nearby office workers. Today the Old Slave Lodge is an important leg on the International Slave Route Project established by Unesco. It also houses the **Cultural History Museum**, which showcases artefacts from around the world.

Iziko South African Museum and Planetarium

25 Queen Victoria Street;

Right: Slave Lodge Museum; South African Museum

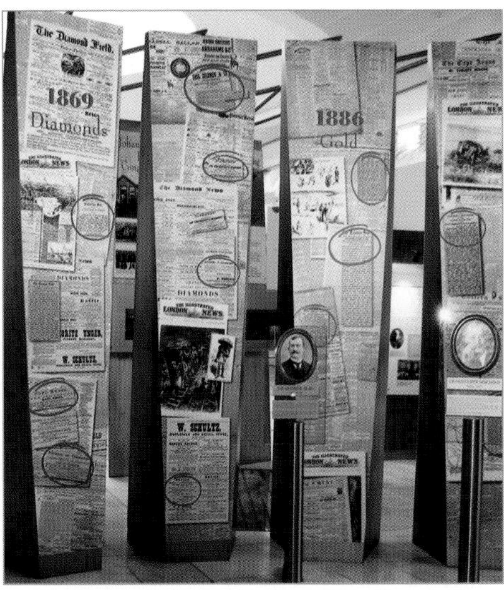

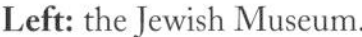

Left: the Jewish Museum.

tel: 021 481 3800/3900; www.iziko.org.za/sam; museum: daily 10am–5pm, planetarium: daily 10am–5pm, shows: Mon–Fri 2pm, Tue 8pm, Sat–Sun noon, 1pm, 2.30pm; entrance charge; map p.136 A3
This fascinating museum has permanent collections on both the natural and the human sciences. There are fossils, rocks and minerals, skeletons of animals, whales, and there's a magnificent collection of South African beadwork and other cultural items from the country's indigenous people. Among the highlights is the mysterious rock art of the San people. Look out for the coelacanth, a prehistoric fish, which was found in the 20th century still to be living off the coast at East London.

The South African sky at night is remarkable; however, city-bound stargazers have the **Planetarium**. Part of the Iziko South African Museum, it has a 'theatre of the stars' projected onto the interior of a huge dome. The wide programme of events includes 'star finder' astronomy courses, changing exhibitions (some designed for children) and field trips to the country to explore the night skies.
SEE ALSO CHILDREN, P.40

Jewish Museum
88 Hatfield Street, Gardens; tel: 021 465 1546; www.sajewishmuseum.co.za; Sun–Thur 10am–5pm, Fri 10am–2pm; entrance charge; map p.136 A3
This striking museum presents a compelling account of the long history of the Jewish community in Cape Town, and stages some of the liveliest temporary exhibitions in town.

The museum incorporates the city's Old Synagogue, recognisable for its classical temple front, built in 1862. The complex also includes the **Cape Town Holocaust Centre** and the **Jacob Gitlin Library**. Next door is the **Great Synagogue**, built in 1904. It wasn't until 1804 that freedom of worship was permitted in the Cape. A large contingent of Jews arrived from Europe in the 1860s, drawn by the discovery of diamonds, and in the 1880s refugees from the pogroms in Russia coincided with the discovery of gold. South Africa has a large Jewish community to this day, and this is its oldest congregation.

The most interesting exhibits in the South African Museum relate to the rock art of the San bushmen, who lived in South Africa until the end of the 19th century and still live in neighbouring Namibia today. Some of the examples here are no more than 200 years old, but are of considerable interest.

Left: the Irma Stern Museum.

The Holocaust Centre is the only one in Africa. With changing exhibits, archival documents and films, tableaux and survivor testimonies, it is a place of remembrance and learning about the disastrous consequences of unchecked racial discrimination.

SEE ALSO CHURCHES, SYNAGOGUES AND MOSQUES, P.42

Koopmans-De Wet House

35 Strand Street; tel: 021 481 3935; www.iziko.org.za/koopmans; Tue–Thur 9am–5pm; entrance charge; map p.136 B2

A small but beautiful two-storey Cape Dutch townhouse of the time when downtown streets were lined with elegant homes. With its mullioned windows, pilasters, classical pediment and magnificent fanlight, it's a perfect example of neoclassical Cape architecture. Inside, look out for the murals depicting architectural details – dados, door cases and plinths. The house was acquired by the De Wet family in 1806, and at the end of the 19th century was inhabited by Mrs Marie Koopmans-De Wet (1834–1906), a socialite who entertained many influential guests while living here. These days it is furnished as a lived-in home in the style of the late 18th-century and houses a first-class collection of early Cape furniture, arranged traditionally, Dutch Delft ceramics, fine porcelain, glass and silverware.

Old Town House

Greenmarket Square, City Centre; tel: 021 481 3933; Mon–Fri 10am–5pm, Sat 10am–4pm; free, but donations welcome; map p.136 A2

A fine historic building dating back to 1761, thought to have been one of the first two-storey buildings in Cape Town. It was in 1917 that the Old Town House first became an art gallery. The interior is extremely handsome, but it's quite unlike anything you would have found in the Cape at the time, and it is a good example of the English Arts and Crafts movement of the late 19th century. The house was subsequently considered to be an appropriate setting for the Michaelis Collection, a large collection of 17th-century Dutch and Flemish paintings amassed and donated by Sir Max Michaelis in 1914. The works include still lifes, portraits and landscapes.

Rust en Vreugd

78 Buitenkant Street; tel: 021 464 3280; www.iziko.org.za/rustvreugd; Tue–Thur 8.30am–4.30pm; free; map p.136 B3

A fine Cape Dutch mansion built in 1777 which has had its garden restored. It also houses the William Fehr Collection of Africana – part of the bigger collection housed in the Castle of Good Hope *(see p.76)*. Drawings, etchings, watercolours and other works depict views and scenes of life in early Cape Town, historical events, and notable people and buildings. Take note of the façade of the building, with its lovely period fanlights, handsome architraves and carved teak doors.

VICTORIA AND ALFRED WATERFRONT AND ROBBEN ISLAND

Robben Island Museum

Ferries depart from the Nelson Mandela Gateway, Clock Tower Precinct, V&A Waterfront;

Right: SA Naval Museum.

Wander the city streets with Footsteps to Freedom (tel: 021 426 4260), starting at the Visitors Information Centre at the corner of Castle and Burg streets. Learn about the Cape's history as you walk through Greenmarket Square, Parliament, District Six Museum and others. The walk takes around three hours, leaving Mon-Fri at 10.30am–1.30pm.

tel: 021 413 4220; www.robben-island.org.za; daily 7am–9pm; ferries 9am, 10am, 11am, noon, 1pm, 2pm, 3pm; entrance charge; map p.133 E3/inside back cover
Jump on a ferry and visit this famous National Heritage site where Nelson Mandela was held captive for 18 years. Arriving on the island, you will board a bus for a guided tour of the prison buildings, graveyards, the remains of an ancient shipwreck, a lime quarry and finally a tour of the island's penguin colony.

SA Maritime Museum
Union Castle Building, V&A Waterfront; tel: 021 405 2880; www.iziko.org.za/maritime; daily 10am–5pm; map p.133 D3
An ode to shipping, this small museum mainly comprises models of historic ships that docked at these shores. Of particular interest is a model of Cape Town's harbour built in 1880 with the help of six prisoners from Breakwater Prison nearby.

BO-KAAP

Bo-Kaap Museum
71 Wale Street; tel: 021 481 3939; www.iziko.org.za/bokaap; Mon–Sat 9am–5pm; entrance charge; map p.136 A2
Once a *huurhuisie* and dating from around 1763, this small museum pays tribute to the people of Bo-Kaap. It also gives some idea of the furnishings of a relatively wealthy 19th-century Cape Muslim family.

All the early woodwork survives, including the original teak windows, teak shutters, the doors and the fanlight above the front door. The museum contains photographs and pictures depicting the lifestyle of the community as well as interesting relics of daily life. In particular, it portrays the devastating effects that Apartheid and the Group Areas Act had on the community. This museum commemorates a community that played a pivotal role in the shaping of Cape Town.

SOUTHERN SUBURBS

Irma Stern Museum
Cecil Road, Rosebank; tel: 021 685 5686; www.irmastern.co.za; Tue–Sat 10am–5pm; entrance charge
Painter, explorer, collector and adventurer Irma Stern (1894–1966) is arguably one of South Africa's most important 20th-century artists. Take a stroll through her home, with its rooms filled with exotic paintings and artefacts, Congolese sculptures and 7th-century Tang figures that fill up the shelves and passages of this restored house.

South African Rugby Museum
Sports Science Institute, Boundary Road, Newlands; tel: 021 686 2151; www.newlandstours.co.za; Mon–Thur 8am–4.30pm, Fri 8am–4pm; free
For those who are serious about rugby, a stroll through this museum takes visitors on a journey through some historic and memorable tries and tackles over the years. Watch snippets of legendary games from the past and enjoy looking at other significant rugby memorabilia on the walls.

CAPE PENINSULA

SA Naval Museum
Naval Dockyard, St George's Street, Simon's Town; tel: 021 787 4686; www.simonstown.com/navalmuseum; daily 9.30am–3.30pm; free
Housed in the Royal Navy's original dockyard magazine with an eclectic array of missiles, torpedos, boats, historical documents and other naval paraphernalia. You can also take a look around the inside of a submarine control room, climb up to the clock

tower or walk to the dockyard church.

Simon's Town Museum
The Residency, Court Road, Simon's Town; tel: 021 786 3046; www.simonstown.com; Mon–Fri 9am–4pm, Sat 10am–1pm, Sun 11am–3pm; entrance charge
This historic residency, built in 1777, was the winter home of the Dutch East India Company Governor to the Cape and is one of the best museums of its kind in South Africa. It's a treasure trove of information which encapsulates the history of the town and its people, and their connection both to the Dutch East India Company and the Royal Navy, in great detail. The museum also arranges guided walks around the more historic parts of the town, including both the mosque and the churches.

The residency was used over the years as a hospital, post office, school, customs house, police station, prison and magistrate's court, and the exhibits reflect the composite functions of this lovely old building. They begin with artefacts relating to the earliest inhabitants of the area, and tools and equipment of the Khoisan people of the South Peninsula are also exhibited. The early history of the Company and van der Stel is well documented. Many of these original buildings have been declared National Monuments.

Warrior Toy Museum and Collectors' Shop
St George's Street, Simon's Town; tel: 021 786 1395; daily 10am–4pm; entrance charge
This is a treasure chest of dolls and doll's houses, dinky toys, model cars, soldiers, trains and old bears. This is a toy-collector's heaven with the catalogue of historic toys on display, and perhaps that rare find you've been searching for.

Art Galleries

CITY CENTRE AND CITY BOWL

34 Long
34 Long Street, City Centre; tel: 021 426 4594; www.34long.com; Tue–Fri 9am–5pm, Sat 10am–2pm; map p.136 B2
Set inside an inspiring space

Right: miniatures at the Warrior Toy Museum.

Left: the Simon's Town Museum.

While in Simon's Town look out for Just Nuisance's grave – a Great Dane who would accompany British World War II seamen on their pub crawls through Cape Town, alerting the drunken officers when the final train was heading back to Simon's Town.

in the form of an old Victorian building in the heart of Long Street, this is where you come to source modern artworks by local heavyweights, namely William Kentridge, Esther Mahlangu and Norman Catherine. A good mix of artworks that will keep you coming back for more. Regular auctions are also held at the gallery if you're in the business for some serious investment art.

3rd I Gallery
95 Waterkant Street, De Waterkant; tel: 021 425 2266; Mon–Fri 9am–5pm, Sat 9.30am–1pm; map p.133 D4
A young and edgy gallery in vibrant De Waterkant featuring a range of different art that adorns the exposed brick walls. A hand-picked choice of landscapes, portraits, installations and other mixed-media pieces are all for sale.

Association for Visual Arts
35 Church Street, City Centre; tel: 021 424 7436; www.ava.co.za; Mon–Fri 10am–5pm, Sat 10am–1pm; map p.136 A2
While you're taking a stroll through the antique market down Church Street, don't forget to pop into this historic exhibition space, which is the oldest non-profit art gallery in Cape Town. It showcases a diverse range of art and media techniques. There is a strong focus on artists from disadvantaged backgrounds who are creating art pieces worth collecting.

Bell-Roberts Gallery
Fairweather House, 176 Sir Lowry Road, Woodstock; tel: 021 465 9108; Mon–Fri 8.30am–5.30pm, Sat 10am-2pm; map p.137 D3
This is considered, by those in the know, as one of the city's foremost creative working hubs in terms of art publishing, art-making and a frame-making venture on the side. A diverse and lively art gallery with regular walk-in exhibitions by local movers and shakers.

Cape Gallery
60 Church Street, City Centre; tel: 021 423 5309; www.capegallery.co.za; Mon–Fri 9.30am–5pm, Sat 10am–2pm; map p.136 A2
A traditional Cape Dutch interior with some of the most inspiring art collections decorating the walls. The selection is mostly traditional landscapes, figurative studies and intricate still lives.

Erdmann Contemporary
63 Shortmarket Street, City Centre; tel: 021 422 2762; www.erdmanncontemporary.co.za; Mon–Fri 10am–5pm, Sat 11am–1pm; map p.136 A2
The Photographers Gallery and the Erdmann Contemporary are both housed in the same light and breezy double-volume premises. Owner Heidi Erdmann has a good eye for local work, and her gallery space is home to some of the best photographic work in South Africa, like that of Lien Botha and Roger Ballen. The gallery also sells specialist books on photography.

Focus Contemporary
2 Long Street, City Centre; tel: 021 419 8888; www.focuscontemporary.co.za; Mon–Fri

9.30am–6pm, Sat 10am–2pm; map p.136 B1

This is a light-filled gallery space always features something newsworthy on its four walls. Owner Migo Manz focuses on the provocative power of photography and its message to viewers. Always a guaranteed visual treat at every monthly exhibition.

Iziko South African National Gallery

Government Avenue, City Centre; tel: 021 467 4660; www.iziko.org.za; Tue–Sun 10am–5pm; entrance charge; map p.136 A3

This small gallery is one of the top showcases of South African art, and it also has an eclectic collection of European works, including British, French, Dutch and Flemish art. Ultimately, though, it's the local paintings, sculpture, ceramics, beadwork and textiles that people come here to see, and for changing exhibitions.

Joao Ferreira Fine Art

70 Loop Street, City Centre; tel: 021 423 5403; www.joaoferreiragallery.com; winter: Tue–Fri 11am–5pm, Sat 11am–2pm, summer: Tue–Fri 11am–6pm, Sat 11am–3pm; map p.136 A2

Art dealer Joao Ferreira has played a major role in spotting rising stars of the art world for many years now. For those wanting to start investing in local art, this is a good place to start.

Michael Stevenson Gallery

Ground Floor, Buchanan Building, 160 Sir Lowry Rd, Woodstock; tel: 021 462 1500; www.michaelstevenson.com; Mon–Fri 9am–5pm, Sat 10am–1pm; map p.137 D3

Left: Iziko South African National Gallery.

This upmarket gallery continues to grow the art market with its professional and intriguing exhibitions. For any art-lover, this is a must-visit. And start saving now – you're guaranteed to want something off the walls or the floor to take home with you.

VICTORIA AND ALFRED WATERFRONT

Die Kunskamer

3 Portswood Square, Lower Portswood Road; tel: 021 419 3226; www.kunskamer.co.za; Mon–Fri 8.30am–5pm, Sat 9.30am–1pm; map p.133 D3

A veteran establishment in the Cape that features some serious heavyweights on the South African art circuit, including names like Irma Stern, Cecil Skotnes and Robert Hodgins.

Everard Read Gallery

3 Portswood Road; tel: 021 418 4527; www.everard-read-capetown.co.za; Mon–Fri 9am–6pm, Sat 9am–1pm; map p.133 D3

This is the Cape Town arm of one of South Africa's oldest commercial art galleries, and some of the local artists on their books are well recognised around the world. The gallery mostly holds classic oil paintings and bronze sculpture, but you can always expect some surprises during the month.

SOUTHERN SUBURBS

What if the World

1st Floor Albert Hall, 208 Albert Road, Woodstock; tel: 021 448 1438; www.whatiftheworld.com; Tue–Fri 10am–4pm, Sat 10am–2pm, Sun by appointment only; map p.137 E3

A new gallery that's on the tip of everybody's tongue, possibly because it's also the energy behind the hugely successful Neighbour Goods Market *(see p.56 and 74)*. Find reasonable and accessible artwork, some done through community upliftment projects.

CAPE PENINSULA

Bronze Age Sculpture House

King George's Way, Simon's Town; tel: 021 786 5090; www.bronzeageart.com; Mon–Thur 8am–4.30pm, Fri 8am–3pm, weekends by appointment only

On the way out of Simon's Town, you may want to call in at the Bronze foundry, gallery and sculpture garden – a wharf-side complex where you can see artists at work. The working foundry is worth taking a look around, and the adjoining gallery displays work by top local artists.

Kalk Bay Gallery

62 Main Road, Kalk Bay; tel: 021 788 1674; www.farsa.co.za; daily 9am–5pm

An intimate little gallery that constantly has an interesting mix of landscapes and abstract works by talented neighbourhood artists and ceramicists (who've all gathered in Kalk Bay over the years) producing some quality art.

Kalk Bay Modern

50 Main Road, Kalk Bay; tel: 021 788 6571; daily 9.30am–5pm

Bohemian, vibrant and always welcoming, the Kalk Bay Modern is an eclectic gallery worth seeing, especially some of the ceramics and crafts on offer.

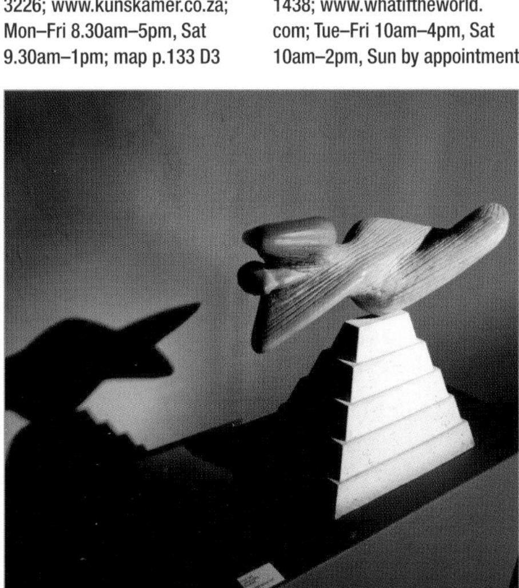

Left: Bronze Age Sculpture House.

Music, Dance and Theatre

Out of the Apartheid era, the horror of the Group Areas Act, forced removals and displaced people, South Africa developed a strong tradition in theatre, arts and music (jazz in particular), as culture was one of the few things the regime struggled to suppress. Cape Town is still a hotbed of creative activity, and options include old-school theatres and concert halls like the Artscape offering old-world entertainment in the form of opera and ballet, jazz bars, open-air concerts in botanical gardens and intimate revue bars.

Music

AFRICAN

Marco's African Place
15 Rose Street, City Centre; tel: 021 423 5412; www.marcosafricanplace.co.za; Tue–Sat noon to late, Sun 3pm to late; map p.136 A1
An African-themed restaurant aimed at the tourist market. Expect some Afro-indigenous sounds and a touch of township jazz. Get ready to beat to some drums too. A thrilling night out on the town.

CLASSICAL AND OPERA

Both the **Cape Town Philharmonic Orchestra** (CPO) and the **Cape Town Opera** have shaken off their fuddy-duddy appeal of old and transformed themselves into world-class companies, appealing to both a young and old audience. They have brought classics to new ears with some innovative and varied collaborations. For more information visit www.cpo.org.za and www.capetownopera.co.za.

City Hall
Darling Street, Grand Parade; tel: 021 410-9809; www.cpo.org.za; map p.136 B2

> Don't miss the Cape Town International Comedy Festival, which takes place during the month of September at the Baxter Theatre, tel: 021 685 7880; www.baxter.co.za. Catch some of South Africa's best stand-up acts, who will keep you in stitches of laughter.

This is where you'll catch the Cape Town Philharmonic Orchestra and Opera in action. This century-old building holds regular, full-house performances of a varied nature with some well-priced tickets. They are known for their excellent quality in sound for non-amplified music.

JAZZ

Cape Jazz is legendary, even though the epicentre of the South African jazz scene has moved up-country to Johannesburg. Catch the **Cape Town International Jazz Festival**, which takes place annually in January.

Dizzy Jazz Café
39 and 41 The Drive, Camps Bay; tel: 021 438 2686; daily noon–3am; free; map p.138 A4
Set back from the Camps Bay strip and its numerous beach bars, Dizzy's brings an alternative to the suburb's obsession with cocktails and canapés with beer, a great pizza menu and regular jazz sets. More friendly than fancy, it's a good option if you prefer your nights out relaxed and rustic.

The Green Dolphin
Victoria and Alfred Arcade, Pierhead, V&A Waterfront; tel: 021 421-7471; www.greendolphin.co.za; daily 8.15pm until late; entrance charge; map p.133 E3
From buskers to impromptu concerts in the open-air theatre, the V&A Waterfront is one of the premier destinations for jazz in Cape Town, and The Green Dolphin is one of its stars. Offers bistro-like food and regular appearances by both internationals and celebrated South African acts. A live-entertainment charge is added to your bill at the end of the evening.

Right: The Green Dolphin jazz bar at the V&A Waterfront.

Left: a production by the Jazzart Dance Theatre *(see p.88)*.

Kirstenbosch Concerts
Rhodes Drive, Newlands; tel: 021 761 2866; www.sanbi.org; Dec–Mar: Sun 5.30pm–8pm
What started off a few years ago as a couple of low-key concerts on the lawns of this famous botanical garden has become a weekly migration as thousands of people flock to Kirstenbosch to catch top local bands like Freshlyground, Johnny Clegg and international acts like Ishmael Lo. What with parking, booking tickets and having to deal with bigger crowds, it's not as relaxing as it was at the beginning, but that's the price of success. Still a great way to spend a summer's Sunday afternoon.

Manenberg's
Shop 102, Ground Level, Clock Tower Centre, V&A Waterfront; tel: 021 421 5639; www.manenbergjazzcafe.com; daily 11.30am to late; entrance charge; map p.133 E3
Though far from the suburb of Manenberg itself, this popular jazz club and the musicians who frequent it evoke the spirit of South Africa in all its dirty glory. Having hosted some of SA's jazz legends like Hugh Masekela, Jabu Khanyile and Zim Nqawana, and with Cabinet ministers and celebs as regulars, you never know who might pop in for an impromptu set.

Marimba
Cape Town International Convention Centre, Corner of Coen Steytler and Heerengracht, Foreshore; tel: 021 418 3366; www.marimbasa.co.za; Thur–Sat 7.30–10.30pm; entrance charge; map p.136 B1
The jazz club/bar attached to the Cape Town International Convention Centre (CTICC), Marimba is the destination of choice after Cape Town's Fashion Week, Whisky Fest, the Book Fair and any number of conferences held throughout the year. Attracting plenty of international conventioneers, expect cheeky prices, a range of accents and a variety of jazz and world music.

Dance

The Mother City is home to some of the most cutting-edge dance companies around: whether contemporary, ballet, fusion, jazz, belly dancing or tap, you're sure to find something. As for performances, the Artscape and the Baxter regularly put on

shows. Check the daily press for details.

Cape Town City Ballet
Artscape Theatre Complex, DF Malan Street, Foreshore; based at UCT School of Dance, Rosebank; tel: 021 650 2400; www.capetowncityballet.org.za; map p.136 C1

This ballet company is the oldest of its kind in Cape Town. Apart from staging some classics like *Carmen* and *The Nutcracker*, the Cape Town City Ballet is also exploring more contemporary-style productions creating a powerful fusion of dance, opera, rock singers, Afro-pop and the Cape Town Philharmonic Orchestra.

Jazzart Dance Theatre
Artscape Theatre Centre, DF Malan Street, Foreshore; tel: 021 410 9848; www.jazzart.co.za; map p.136 C1

While this dance company offers training in African dance (gumboot and contemporary), it's worth making a note of the fund-raiser production that they put together every year, called Danscape at the Artscape Theatre. It features mostly community dance groups who are still in training, and gives them the chance to get some on-stage performing experience.

> Bookings for most productions can be made online through computicket, www.computicket.co.za, and through Dial-a-Seat, tel: 021 421 7695/ 021 421 7839.

Theatre

The theatre scene in Cape Town caters for a mix of tastes and flavours. If you're looking for mincing drag queens or contemporary theatre spots, there are a wide selection of shows and extraordinary venues to match the performances, like old churches, post offices and even the old zoo.

Artscape Theatre Centre
DF Malan Street, Foreshore; tel: 021 410 9800; www.artscape.co.za; box office Mon–Fri 9am–5pm, Sat 9.30am–12.30pm; map p.136 C1

The Cape's massive multicultural old maid (14,000sq metres/17,000sq yds), the Artscape plays host to everything from drama, ballet and opera in its opera house, theatre and arena theatre. The imposing building is itself often used for international film sets and music videos.

Baxter Theatre
Main Road, Rondebosch; tel: 021 685 7880; www.baxter.co.za; box office Mon–Sat 9am–start of show

With a theatre, a concert hall and a studio theatre, the Baxter (which is connected to the University of Cape Town) is Cape Town's second-biggest theatre after the Artscape. With an ever-changing bill containing everything from live theatre to music, dance and comedy, it has played host to absolute unknowns and bigger names like Richard E. Grant, John Kani and Anthony Sher.

Kalk Bay Theatre
52 Main Road, Kalk Bay; tel: 073 220 5430; www.kbt.co.za; Tue–Sun

An excellent option for a night out, this intimate 78-seater coastal theatre situ-

Left: the Baxter Theatre.

ated in a converted historic church plays to one-man acts and small plays and musicals. Book dinner in the upstairs section which looks down on the stage and afterwards mingle with the actors while enjoying your dessert. Booking essential.

Maynardville Open-Air Theatre
Corner of Wolfe and Church streets; tel: 021 421 7695; www.maynardville.co.za; shows Jan–Feb
Responsible for aiding thousands of Cape schoolchildren with their Shakespeare homework due to vastly reduced rates for students, Maynardville is a firm favourite with the theatre set, especially in summer months. A 720-seater open-air theatre set in Maynardville Park, it is renowned for its Shakespeare productions but also features opera and ballet performances.

On Broadway
88 Shortmarket Street, City Centre; tel: 021 424 1194; www.onbroadway.co.za; daily, box office closes 8.30pm; map p.136 A2
You're guaranteed an intimate inner-city dinner theatre/revue bar experience at On Broadway. Big on one-man or one-woman shows, stand-up and musicals. The menu consists of light meals, but the entertainment is hearty.

Theatre @ the Pavilion
1st Floor, BMW Pavilion, Corner of Portswood and Beach roads, V&A Waterfront; tel: 021 419 7661; www.thepavilion.co.za; box office Mon–Wed 8am–5pm, Thur–Sat 8am–8pm; map p.133 D2
Cape Town's old IMAX cinema has been revamped into a state-of-the-art entertainment venue. The focus is on musical tribute shows and stand-up comedy acts. There is a theatre café section where you can grab a quick bite to eat before the show starts.

Theatre on the Bay
1a Link Street, Camps Bay; tel: 021 438 3301; www.theatreonthebay.co.za; box office daily 9.30am–6pm; map p.138 A4
Focusing on smaller shows, cabaret, musicals and dance acts, Camps Bay's Theatre on the Bay gives a more intimate cultural experience than the larger theatres like the Artscape and the Baxter. It also offers dinner before and after the show. Get your interval drinks order in quickly at Dietrich's bar.

Right: the lights are much brighter there...

Nightlife

With stunning scenery and a smorgasbord of bars and restaurants to choose from, Cape Town's a city made for alfresco living. But what happens when the sun goes down? As it happens, plenty. Cosmopolitan, classy, grungy or pick-up joints, Cape Town has them all. From a burgeoning live-music scene, featuring local and foreign acts in every music genre from rock to funk, hip-hop and other indefinable categories, to the late-night glamour clubs where top DJs play to packed out, dressed-up audiences, There are plenty of options; all you have to do is venture out. *See also Bars, p.30–5,* and *Gay and Lesbian, p.58–9.*

DJ Bars and Clubs

The Assembly
61 Harrington Street, District Six, City Centre; tel: 021 426 4552; hours vary; entrance charge; map p.136 B3
Cape Town's premier live music venue in a renovated factory in Cape Town's east city. A big space, it accommodates every crowd from emo, punk, hip-hop to new rave plus visiting international acts and comedy.

The Bang Bang Club
70 Loop Street, City Centre; tel: 021 426 2011; www.thebangbangclub.co.za; Fri–Sat 9pm–4am; entrance charge; map p.136 A2
The sister establishment to swanky beach bar Caprice, the Bang Bang Club (or BBC) is run by a team who have plenty of South African nightclub and DJ experience. This swanky and elegant late-night venue is a destination for dancing, schmoozing and partying the night away. Frequented by a well-dressed, moneyed crowd; dress up or stick out. It gets busy from 10pm until late.

Left and below: The Bang Bang Club.

Venues come and go in Cape Town, but if you're lying on the beach or having a cheeky cocktail at a trendy bar, you are sure to receive a flyer or booklet of what's hot and happening on the club scene. For more information on what's on, check out www.capetownmagazine.com or www.mg.co.za; www.e-vent.co.za; www.thunda.com; www.rage.co.za or www.3am.co.za for updated party calendars and events.

Left: The Assembly is the best place to catch some live music while in Cape Town.

Bronx Action Bar
20 Somerset Road, Green Point; tel: 021 419 9216; www.bronx.co.za; daily 8pm to late; free; map p.133 D4
Oh so gay and oh so proud of it, Bronx is one of the longest-standing pink clubs in Cape Town. Situated on Somerset Road, the city's Pink Mile, Bronx offers DJs (Tuesdays to Sundays) playing banging tunes late into the early morning, karaoke on Mondays and a very friendly crowd intent on hooking up.

Chrome Night Club
6 Pepper Street, City Bowl; tel: 083 700 6078; www.chromect.com; Wed–Sat 9pm–4am; entrance charge; map p.136 A2
A pretentious club that buys into all the nightclub clichés of VIP sections, velvet ropes, a VIP list, a painfully slow queue and a cover charge. Perfect if that's your thing.

Deco Dance
375 Albert (Lower Main) Road, Salt River; tel: 084 330 1162; www.decodance.co.za; Fri–Sat 9pm until late; entrance charge
At the Old Biscuit Mill – the venue for Cape Town's hugely successful Neighbour Goods Market *(see p.74)* and home to a host of boutique stores – if you take a short stroll towards the old silo of the mill, you could disappear through a trapdoor and reappear in the cheesy '80s rock pit that is Deco Dance. Weird cock-pit like seating, a chequered dance floor and a crowd dedicated to hanging onto memories of the '80s will bring out your inner Bowie.

Fiction
226 Long Street, City Centre; tel: 021 424 5709; www.fictionbar.com; Tue–Sat 8pm–4am; entrance charge; map p.136 B1
Decorated in a retro comic book, video game and cult movie theme, this very popular club is at the business end of Long Street. Its small

but packed dance floor attracts a loyal crowd of trendy locals with interesting haircuts. The balcony is great for checking out the rest of Long Street, but the restrooms are small and wholly inadequate for the crowd flooding into Fiction on busy nights. Usually quiet until 10pm, when things pick up.

FTV

114 Hout Street, Corner of Buitengracht Street; tel: 021 426 6000; www.ftv.com; Wed, Fri, Sat, 8pm–4am; entrance charge; map p.136 A2

Part of a chain where the young and pretty go to look at, well, other young and pretty things, FTV is a slightly contrived yet successful formula. TVs play Fashion TV in the background while the dance floor is kept busy with models, wannabees working on their pouts and all that's in between. Wednesdays are busy.

Ignite

2nd Level, The Promenade, Camps Bay; tel: 021 438 7717; www.ignitebar.co.za; Thur–Sat 9pm–2am; entrance charge; map p.138 A3

Camps Bay strip's premier spot for when you want to segue from sipping sundowners to dancing and shooters. Theoretically, you wouldn't have to move if you began your evening here. Start with sundowners or cocktails amongst the tanned and toned locals and foreigners and, as the evening progresses and the drinks flow, move onto the dance floor for what is billed as higher-grade hip-hop. Thursdays are Ignite's premier evening.

Karma

Penthouse Suites, The Promenade, Camps Bay; tel: 021 438 7773; www.karmalounge.co.za; Wed–Sat 5pm–2am; map p.138 A3

Camps Bay's Karma is fun with two bars, a dance floor and a couple of alcoves and balconies for you to catch your breath. Karma is also the resident club for the Global Breakthrough DJ confederacy which plays on Saturday nights.

Above: take a breather on the balconies at Karma; **left and right:** Long Street's Fiction bar.

L/B's

222 Long Street, City Centre; tel: 021 422 0142; private parties weekly; entrance charge; map p.136 B1

With a circular lounge and bar trimmings that are both retro and space-age, it looks as though L/B's was designed for Dr Evil and his cohorts – which is perfect if you have a yen for cheesy dancing. Upstairs from Long Street stalwart Joburg, L/B's is a good option, probably one of the best nights out in Cape Town, especially when The Wedding DJs are on the decks.

Tiger Tiger

Stadium on Main, Claremont Main Road, Southern Suburbs; tel: 021 683 2220; www.tigertiger.co.za; Tue–Sat 9pm–4am; entrance charge

A meat market for the young and restless, Tiger Tiger is a moving club that started in Durban, moved to Johannesburg and now pumps out of Cape Town's Claremont suburb. Frequented by students, young rat-racers and anyone else looking for a big night out, the drinks are cheap, the music loud and everyone is on display (the dance floor is in a sunken pit into which wallflowers watch).

Wadda

14 Stegman Road, Claremont, Southern Suburbs; tel: 021 683 7700; www.wadda.co.za; Mon, Wed, Sat 9pm–4am; entrance charge

A classy, upbeat and upmarket venue with two levels, three bars and a VIP room where one can rest one's tired stilettoed feet. Mostly a student venue luring in a yuppie Southern Suburbs clique, but always lots of fun. Check out its website for a line-up of resident DJs during the week.

Always make sure that you have organised transport home, as drink-driving in South Africa is illegal and could land you in jail for the night. Make every effort to take official metered taxis at night, which usually hang around outside the club's entrance, and try to travel in a group (especially women). Public transport on buses, trains or in a minibus after dark is not recommended.

Pampering

If you're feeling in need of some me-time after a packed sightseeing schedule, why not check yourself into one of Cape Town's finest luxury spas, retreats or wellness centres for a bit of well-deserved rejuvenation. If you're looking to be pampered, pummelled, polished or plumped, most packages can be tailor-made to suit your individual needs. Just breathe in deeply, unwind and enjoy some star treatment – you're guaranteed to leave feeling healthy, energised and in the pink. The spas and beauty salons listed below come recommended and are just the tip of the iceberg.

Spas

Angsana Spa
Vineyard Hotel, Colinton Road, Newlands; tel: 021 674 5005; www.angsanaspa.com; daily 8am–8pm
Managed and created by the award-winning Banyan Tree Spa Team, here excellent Thai therapists offer treatments ranging from indulgent facials and pedicures to more intense massage therapy using fragrant essential oils.

Arabella Spa
Westin Grand Cape Town, Arabella Quays, 1 Lower Long Street, Convention Square; tel: 021 412 9999; www.westin.com/capetown; daily 8am–7pm; map p.136 B1
If you're staying in the city, head for the 19th floor of the Westin Grand hotel and experience this sky-high, newly revamped spa with views of the harbour and bustling city below. Be rubbed, scrubbed, oiled and pampered in the peace and tranquillity of this modern space.

Camelot Spa
Table Bay Hotel, V&A Waterfront; tel: 021 406 5904; www.camelotspagroup.com; daily 7.30am–9pm; map p.133 E2
A classic day spa on the Waterfront that offers great pick-me-up treatments. Try an Ayurvedic treatment using marine-based Thalgo products to get your senses going.

Glasshouse
Unit 110A, The Foundry, 74 Prestwich Street, Green Point; tel: 021 419 9599/8; Mon 9am–7pm, Tue–Thur 9am–8pm, Fri 9am–7pm, Sat 9am–5pm; map p.133 D4
For men-on-the-go wanting a little head-to-toe grooming in slick (and manly) surroundings, this urban spa for men does everything from waxing and bronzing to massage and hot towel shaves. Have a pedicure whilst sipping on an icy beer or a cappucino and surf the sport channels on their plasma TV.

Librisa Spa
Mount Nelson Hotel, 76 Orange Street, Gardens; tel: 021 483 1550; www.librisa.co.za; daily 9am–8pm; map p.135 E3
For complete indulgence head for the newly opened Librisa Spa at the Mount Nelson *(see p.63)*. Situated in a cluster of old heritage homes, this slick day spa has been turned into an exquisite two-level sanctuary. Décor is contemporary yet warm, with state-of-the-art finishes. An invigorating and fully energising experience.

Onewellness
Radisson SAS Waterfront, Beach Road, Granger Bay, V&A Waterfront, tel: 021 441 3331/2/3; www.onewellness.co.za; daily 6am–10pm; map p.133 D2
Spend your day lounging around the pool wrapped in your long kimono robe and enjoy full access to all the spa facilities as well as treatments using modern and traditional techniques.

Paris Spa
Shop 13, Wembley Square, Solan Street, Gardens; tel: 021 462 0021; www.parisspa.co.za; daily 7am–9pm; map p.136 B4
Décor is clean and simple, with soft lighting and pebbled floors. Treatments are based on the ancient ritual of steam baths and massage with a modern take on how to stimulate the senses. Leave feeling glowing and thoroughly glamorous.

Left: the Sanctuary Spa at the Twelve Apostles hotel.

If you're looking for the perfect health resort, medi-spa, wellness centre, hydro, health or pamper spa, visit www.healthspas.co.za for a comprehensive list of nearly 30 spas in Cape Town and 50 in the Western Cape.

Sanctuary Spa
The Twelve Apostles, Victoria Road, Camps Bay; 021 437 0677; www.12apostleshotel.com; daily 9am–9pm; map p.138 A3
This is the perfect spa getaway, just a short drive out of town. Situated inside a grotto-like space with flotation pools, this Eastern-inspired spa offers a range of different therapies (they have a Rasul chamber too) and beauty treatments. A new addition are the outdoor treatment rooms overlooking the sea.

Skincare Shops

The Body Shop
Shop G54, Ground Floor, Cavendish Square; tel: 021 671 1082; www.thebodyshop.co.za; Mon–Sat 9am–7pm; Sun 10am–5pm
With stores dotted around the country, you can stock up on a fruit salad of great-smelling body products and an excellent make-up offering.

M.A.C Cosmetics
Shop 6140, Ground Floor, Victoria Wharf; tel: 021 421 4886; www.maccosmetics.com; Mon–Sat 9am–9pm, Sun 10am–9pm; map p.133 E2
This is where you'll find the glam girl about town filling up her make-up bag with everything from eyeshadow and lip gloss in the latest fashion colours to powders, creams and other must-have paraphernalia.

Specialist Beauty Treatments

Chelsea Aesthetic Centre
51A Waterloo Road, Wynberg; tel: 021 797 5001/7066; www.chelseaspa.co.za; Mon 7am–5.30pm, Tue–Thur 7am–9pm, Fri 7am– 6.30pm, Sat 8am–5.30pm, Sun 8.30am–5pm
This is a small, chic salon in a fabulously renovated Victorian house in Chelsea Village. Treatments include everything from wraps and facials to non-surgical facelifts and pigmentation therapy.

Renaissance Body Science Institute
183 Bree Street; tel: 021 486 8840; www.renaissancebsi.co.za; daily 8am–5pm; map p.136 A2
This is a one-stop shop for those in need of an extreme makeover. Image consultant, plastic surgeon, dentist, nutritionist, personal trainers and a beauty spa.

Right: the Angsana Spa is situated at the Vineyard Hotel.

Parks and Reserves

Surrounded by a sprawling national park and a mountainous spine stretching from Signal Hill in the north to Cape Point in the south, nowhere else in the world does a wilderness with such startling biodiversity exist within a city housing some 3 million people. There are also several national parks and reserves around the Cape Peninsula and further afield that are recognised globally for their extraordinarily rich, diverse and unique flora and fauna, rugged cliffs and steep slopes. *See also Walks and Views, p.126–9.*

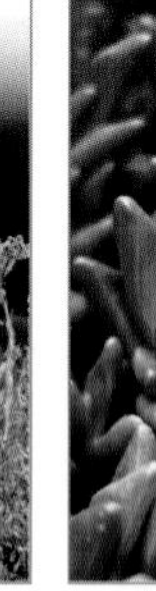

City Centre

Company's Garden
Government Avenue, enter via Adderley Street; daily 8am–dusk; map p.136 A3
Right at the heart of the city, the Company's Garden is all that survives of the original 18-hectare (44-acre) vegetable garden laid out by the Dutch East India Company and developed as a source of fresh fruit and vegetables for their ships as they passed by on their way between Europe and the East.

Now a botanical garden and public park, it has more than 8,000 species of trees and plants, plus a fernery, a palm grove, a herb garden, a fuchsia house and a conservatory.

Table Mountain National Park
Also accessible from Southern Suburbs; tel: 021 712 7471; www.sanparks.org; fees for Cape of Good Hope, Boulders and Silvermine; map p.132–9
Since 1988, the Table Mountain National Park (TMNP), including famous landmarks like **Devil's Peak**, **Lion's Head** and **Signal Hill**, has been extended to include about 72 percent of the entire Cape Peninsula, all the way to Cape Point in the south. Everywhere you look, there are vast panoramas with beautiful valleys, well-watered ravines, sandy flats (like hilltop beaches), and rugged cliffs. It is primarily an open-access park, alhough conservation entrance fees are required at the **Cape of**

> The Table Mountain National Park continues to establish partnerships with the many previously disadvantaged neighbouring communities, creating employment and educating people about caring for the environment, all the while looking at the paucity of water resources, conservation strategies where development cannot be avoided, and management of the landscape.

Left: admiring the Bowl from Table Mountain National Park.

The Otter Trail, which follows the coast all the way from Storms River to Nature's Valley, is renowned as one the most scenic and challenging hikes in South Africa. The 41km (25-mile) trek takes five days (sleeping in huts along the way) and crosses 11 rivers – sometimes you will need to swim rather than just wade. Only 12 people are allowed to start the trail daily, and because it is so popular it should be booked through South African National Parks (www.sanparks.org) up to 13 months in advance.

Left: Kirstenbosch National Botanical Gardens.

Good Hope, **Boulders** and **Silvermine** reserves. There are also various camps where you can overnight should you want to be that little bit closer to nature.

Southern Suburbs

Kirstenbosch National Botanical Gardens

Rhodes Drive, Newlands; tel: 021 799-8783; www.sanbi.org; Sept–May: daily 8am–7pm, June–Aug: daily 8am–6pm; entrance charge

This 528-hectare (1,320-acre) estate at the foot of Table Mountain is home to a diverse range of fynbos (a scrubland indigenous to the Western Cape) and other indigenous flora and fauna. With 36 hectares (89 acres) under cultivation (established in 1913), the gardens only feature plants indigenous to South Africa and are one of the most important botanical collections in the world. It's also one of the best places to spot birds. Look for the glorious orange-breasted Cape sugarbird.

Cape Peninsula

Cape of Good Hope Nature Reserve

Cape Point; tel: 021 465 8515; www.capepoint.co.za; Oct–Mar: daily 6am–6pm, Apr–Sept: daily 7am–5pm; entrance charge

Busloads of tourists flock here every day of the year to see the southernmost tip of the Cape Peninsula. After walking up to the viewing deck, take a stroll on the mountain path among antelopes, elands, zebra, baboons and smaller creatures. See an extensive variety of plant species, and a number of shipwrecks, lighthouses and old cannons. Accommodation is available in secluded self-catering cottages. Visit the Buffelsfontein Visitor Centre in the reserve for more information on walks, hikes and historic sights. Just a reminder not to feed the baboons, as they may appear friendly, but can harm you.

Silvermine Nature Reserve

Ou Kaapse Weg; tel: 021 780 9002; www.tmnp.co.za; Apr–Sept: daily 8am–5pm, Oct–Mar: daily 7am–6pm; entrance charge

This is a sprawling reserve which offers a variety of walking and hiking trails tailored to all ages and abilities. There's also a wheelchair-friendly boardwalk that circles the reservoir and has picnic and *braai* (barbecue) sites dotted around the water's edge. The reserve is popular amongst mountain-bikers and rock-climbers. Hikers can also stay the night in luxury tented camps constructed from alien vegetation sourced in the park, and have porters to carry all luggage.

Cape Winelands

Hottentots Holland Nature Reserve

Also accessible from the Overberg; tel: 021 426 0723; www.capenature.org.za; daily 7am–7pm

This 42,000-hectare (105,000-acre) reserve stretches from Elgin in the south to beyond Villiersdorp in the north, and from the Stellenbosch Mountains in the west, eastwards to the Groenland Mountains. The entrance to the reserve is at **Nuweberg** on the Viljoen's

Pass between Grabouw and Villiersdorp. The main attractions here are the magnificent mountains (with altitudes ranging from 500 metres/1,640ft to 1,590 metres/5.216ft), indigenous flora and fauna and a selection of glistening natural pools one can cool off in. The Cape mountain leopard also roams these areas, but is seldom seen.

Jonkershoek Nature Reserve

Stellenbosch; tel: 021 426 0723; www.capenature.org.za; daily 7am–7pm

Approximately 9km (5½ miles) from Stellenbosch, take a slow, winding drive up the Jonkershoek Road past well-known vineyards and eventually you'll reach the picturesque Jonkershoek Nature Reserve (which also includes a portion of the Assegaaibosch Nature Reserve). With the Jonkershoek Mountains as an arresting backdrop, this is the ideal reserve for keen hikers. For those wanting something less strenuous, **Assegaaibosch** is best for nature trails and family-friendly picnics. The natural vegetation is mostly mountain fynbos, although large pine plantations are a key feature in the valley. You may be lucky and spot some raptors, but beware of spitting cobras basking in the sun on hot days. The lower reaches of the valley are also a well-known wine-producing area.

Karoo Desert National Botanical Garden

Worcester; tel: 023 347 0785; www.sanbi.org; daily 7am–6pm; free, with the exception of the flowering months from Aug–Oct

Karoo Desert National Botanical Garden displays one of the largest collections of indigenous succulents in the southern hemisphere. The best time to visit is in spring, after the winter rains, when a carpet of brightly coloured desert vygies come into bloom. There are a number of plant trails to choose from. Don't miss some of the gardens featuring plant species used once by the bushmen for their medicinal properties. This extraordinary explosion of colour usually occurs around mid-August until the end of September.

Paarl Mountain Nature Reserve

Jan Phillips Mountain Drive, Paarl; tel: 021 872 3658; daily 7am–7pm

The adjacent Paarl Mountain Nature Reserve's trio of lunar domes can be reached via a relatively easy walking trail through slopes draped in protea-studded fynbos. A relatively modern landmark, set on the southern slopes of Paarl Mountain, is the obelisk-like **Afrikaans Taal Monument** (Language Monument), which was erected in 1975 to commemorate the Strooidakkerk (Thatched Roof Church), which was consecrated in 1805.

> For those exploring the parks and reserves around the Peninsula, there are pleasant picnic spots located at the Signal Hill lookout, The Glen, Van Riebeeck Park, Newlands Forest, the Kirstenbosch Botanical Gardens, Constantia Nek, Oudekraal, Tokai, Witsand, Soetwater, Buffels Bay, Bordjiesrif, Miller's Point and Perdekloof.

Right: Karoo Desert National Botanical Garden.

Left: Paarl Mountain Nature Reserve. **Right:** the Harold Porter National Botanical Gardens.

Overberg

Bontebok National Park

Swellendam; tel: 028 514 2735; www.sanparks.org; daily entrance charge

Just 6km (4 miles) south of Swellendam, the Bontebok National Park is home to graceful bontebok, a fynbos-endemic antelope that was hunted to near extinction in the early part of the 20th century, as well as springbok and the rare Cape mountain zebra. Set against the majestic Langeberg Mountains, this reserve is a World Heritage Site, and promotes biodiversity conservation, from the endangered fynbos veld type and coastal Renosterveld to the namesake bontebok. There are also over 200 remarkable bird species.

De Hoop Nature Reserve

East of Bredasdorp; tel: 021 426 0723; www.capenature.org.za; daily 7am–6pm; entrance charge

De Hoop Nature Reserve is approximately 34,000 hectares (85,000 acres) in size and is a weekend hot spot for the adventurous – from hikers and cyclists to bird- and whale-watchers during the winter and early summer. This area is also noted by global conservationists and marine scientists for the **De Hoop Marine Protected Area**, one of the largest marine protected areas in Africa, which provides a sanctuary for a vast and fascinating array of marine life. Here you'll find over 250 different fish species as well as dolphins, seals and Southern right whales (between May and December). Boasting over 86 mammal species, you're guaranteed to see the shy Cape mountain zebra, eland, grey rhebuck, baboon, yellow mongoose, caracal and the rare bontebok.

Fernkloof Nature Reserve

Hermanus; tel: 028 313 8100; www.fernkloof.com; daily 7am–7pm

The 1,400-hectare (3,459-acre) Fernkloof Nature Reserve, on the northern outskirts of Hermanus, protects the pretty fynbos-strewn slopes of the Kleiniviersberg, and is criss-crossed with a rewarding network of day trails.

Harold Porter National Botanical Gardens

Betty's Bay; tel: 028 272 9311; www.sanbi.org; Mon–Fri 8am–4.30pm, Sat–Sun 8am–5pm; entrance charge

This popular botanical garden is about an hour's drive from Cape Town and the perfect day trip for dedicated nature-lovers. Mostly surrounded by rich coastal fynbos (with salt-adapted plants), the gardens encompass mountain slopes covered in wind swept

Left: Knysna Elephant Park.

grasses as well as rocky gorges, waterfalls, natural pools, forests and wetlands littered with ericas, proteas, restios and other bright indigenous bulbs. One can access the beach over sand dunes. Remember to take ample water supplies if you're taking a day trail or hike.

Kogelberg Biosphere Reserve

Kleinmond; tel: 028 271 5138; www.capenature.org.za; daily 8am–7pm; entrance charge

For dedicated hikers and botanists, the vast Kogelberg Biosphere Reserve is said to protect the most diverse montane fynbos habitat in the Cape, with more than 1,500 plant species identified, a full 10 percent of which occur nowhere else. The reserve also harbours a wide variety of birds, a healthy Chama baboon population and a herd of wild horses, probably descended from beasts abandoned by soldiers of unknown affinities in the Anglo-Boer War of 1899–1902. Four hiking trails run through the reserve, from 6km (4 miles) to 23km (14 miles) in length, and there's canoeing on the Palmiet River.

Garden Route

Featherbed Nature Reserve

Knysna; tel: 044 382 1693/7; www.featherbed.co.za; ferry departs daily at 10am, 11.15am, 12.30pm (lunch included), 8.45am, 2.30pm (lunch excluded)

A privately owned nature reserve and South African Heritage Site that's home to the shy Blue duiker, various birds and the endangered Knysna sea horse. Accessible by ferry only; enjoy a four-hour eco-experience and a sumptuous buffet lunch afterwards.

Keurbooms Nature Reserve

Nature's Valley; tel: 044 532 7876; www.capenature.org.za; daily 8am–6pm; entrance charge

Another scenic gem, which lies along the N2 about 7km (4 miles) east of the town centre, immediately before it crosses a bridge over the forest-fringed Keurbooms River. Ferry cruises run along the river three times daily, and it's also possible to follow a hiking trail into the spectacular wooded gorge. But for those who have the time and the energy, there is no better way to explore this reserve than to take one of the canoe trips that overnight at a rustic riverside hut deep in the forested gorge. The tourist office in Plettenberg Bay has all the details.

> Whilst visiting the **Wilderness National Park**, the Half-Collared Kingfisher Trail is a good one to begin with, an 8km (5-mile) circuit that leads through riparian woodland fringing the Touws River to an attractive waterfall that tumbles over a group of gigantic round boulders.

Knysna Elephant Park

Between Knysna and Plettenberg Bay; tel: 044 532 7732; www.knysnaelephantpark.co.za; daily 8.30am–4.30pm; entrance charge

About 10km (6 miles) west of Plettenberg Bay on the Knysna Road, this park protects the few survivors of the wild herds that once roamed these coastal forests, and offers the opportunity to touch and feed a few semi-domesticated tuskers relocated from elsewhere in the country.

Robberg Nature Reserve

Near Plettenberg Bay; tel: 044 533 2125; www.capenature.org.za; daily 7am–5pm; entrance charge

The centrepiece of the reserve is the Robberg ('seal mountain') Peninsula, where dramatic cliffs rise almost vertically from the choppy blue sea, interspersed with several small sandy coves. A full trek circuit covers an undulating 11km (7 miles), but shorter variations are available. The peninsula is home to an impressive colony of Cape fur seals – along with marine birds such as the African black oystercatcher. Look out, too, for

Right: Wilderness National Park.

the whales and dolphins that pass by seasonally.

Tsitsikamma National Park

Near Plettenberg Bay; tel: 042 281 1607; www.sanparks.org; daily 7am–7pm; entrance charge

From Plettenberg Bay you can take either the fairly straight N2 toll road through forests and across the high coastal plain, or the byway (the R102) winding down past the Grootrivier and Bloukrans gorges and through sleepy Nature's Valley on the western boundary of the Tsitsikamma National Park. **Nature's Valley** is a tiny forested village overlooking a wonderfully isolated beach that remains practically undeveloped for tourism – there are few more attractive places to pitch a tent than at the magical National Park campsite on the edge of town.

Taking the back road is a rewarding experience, sinking deep into the forest's cool microclimate. Beneath giant yellowwoods, the shaded floor is thick with proteas, arum lilies and watsonia; vividly coloured lourie birds dart through the dense forest canopy, while shy duiker and bushbuck hide in the undergrowth. Back on the N2, the concrete bridges over the Storms, Groot and Bloukrans rivers were once the biggest such structures in the world.

> The well-run **Storms River Rest Camp**, in the Tsitsikamma National Park 1.5km (1 mile) west of the river mouth, has chalet lodgings and campsites, and forms a good base for swimming, snorkelling and hiking. The short walk from the rest camp to the bridge across the river mouth is a must (look out for seals below the bridge), and you can ascend from here to a viewpoint on the surrounding cliffs.

Either option – the N2 or the R102 – will bring you to the turn-off to **Storms River Mouth**, with its forests and unspoilt, rocky shore, its log cabins and intimidating suspension bridge at the eastern border of the national park. Stretching 35km (20 miles) between Nature's Valley and Storms River, this scenic park protects coastal lagoons, dunes, cliffs, beaches and coral reefs, with an interior of steep ravines, thickly clothed with ancient yellowwoods up 50 metres (164ft) high.

Wilderness National Park

Wilderness; tel: 044 877 1197; www.sanparks.org; daily 7am–5pm; entrance charge

This park protects a series of freshwater pans – the largest are Swartvlei, Langvlei, Groenvlei and Rondevlei – connected by various tributaries of the Touws River, which empties into the ocean in the town. It's a beautiful park, and the combination of open waterways, reed-beds and marshes provides a rich source of food and varied habitats for a wide array of birdlife, as does the surrounding bush and forest. Pink flamingos drift across the shimmering water, straining the surface for tiny algae and crustaceans, and African spoonbills rake the mud with their broad, flat beaks. Of the 95 waterbird species recorded in South Africa, 75 have been seen here.

Understandably popular with birdwatchers, Wilderness National Park also offers some great rambling opportunities in the form of a network of non-strenuous day trails, each of which is named for one of the park's six kingfisher species. A similar route can be followed on the water by renting a canoe from the main rest camp and paddling gently upstream to the base of the falls.

Restaurants

Cape Town is a melting pot of global flavours with award-winning restaurants and chefs that easily stand up to some of the best in the world. There's a plethora of dining options, from casual bistros and neighbourhood pizzerias to hip and happening haute cuisine and Asian tapas. The scenery also allows for some fantastic backdrops – few dining experiences are as satisfying as freshly caught seafood and a glass of icy Sauvignon Blanc overlooking the ocean. Make sure you sample at least one traditional Cape Malay or African dish while you're here, just to complete an unforgettable gastronomic tour of the city.

City Centre

95 Keerom

95 Keerom Street; tel: 021 422 0765; www.95keerom.com; $$$; Mon–Fri noon–2.30pm, Mon–Sat 7–10.30pm; map p.136 A2

A high-design dining experience with an authentic Italian menu prepared by the suave chef-patron Giorgio Nava. It is smart, cool and fashionable, attracting high-profile editors, film stars, bankers and rich Italians. The food is simply prepared yet mouth-watering; fresh line fish with mashed potato, tuna carpaccio, butternut and ricotta ravioli with burnt butter and sage sauce, and so on.

Aubergine

39 Barnet Street, Gardens; tel: 021 465 4909; $$$; Wed–Fri noon–2pm, Mon–Sat 5–10.30pm; map p.136 A3

Prices for two-course meal per person with a half-bottle of house wine:
$ under R150
$$ R150–R200
$$$ R200–R300
$$$$ more than R300

The perfect venue to be wined and dined for a special occasion. A classic and contemporary mix of flavours prepared by chef-patron Harald Bresselschmidt, with a superb wine list (and knowledgeable sommelier to help you choose that perfect bottle). Atmosphere is warm and cosy – a great spot for winter dining.

Birds Boutique Café

127 Bree Street; tel: 021 426 2534; $; Mon–Fri 8am–5pm; map p.136 A2

As you enter this quirky café, it feels like you've just stepped inside an aviary with bird songs quietly chirping in the background. Sit at long wooden communal tables and tuck into a healthy breakfast, or choose from a variety of home-baked cakes and treats. The chocolate-studded muffin is heavenly. The salads and soups are fresh, organic, generously sized and served in artsy ceramic bowls that you'll want to take home with you.

Bizerca

15 Anton Anreith Street, off Jetty Street; tel: 021 418 0001; $$–$$$; Mon–Fri 7am–10.30am, noon–3pm,

Right: Fork on Long Street.

Left: The Tasting Room, Franschhoek, Cape Winelands.

Serious foodies may want to pick up a copy of *Rossouw's Restaurants*, an annual guide to restaurants around most of the country, featuring the opinion of patrons rather than critics.

Left: enjoy top-quality Indian food at Bukhara.

6.30pm–10pm, Sat 6.30pm–10pm; map p.136 B1
Situated in the hub of the banking district in the City Centre, this newly opened bistro offers an exotic menu featuring dishes like sweetbreads and pig's trotters. However, there's lots more to choose from off its ever-changing chalkboard menu, mostly French classics like a scrumptious beef bourgignon and a fine-crust apple tart. It has a varied wine list featuring the usual Cape classics and some exciting newcomers on the wine scene. Interiors are minimal yet warm, and the service is extremely personable, with the owners working the floor and the crowds until closing.

Bukhara
33 Church Street; tel: 021 424 0000; www.bukhara.com; $$$; daily noon–3pm, Tue–Sat 6–11pm; map p.136 A2
Possibly the best curry restaurant in town, Bukhara is noisy and busy, so be sure to make a reservation. The food is authentic and delicious – a house favourite is the succulent butter chicken served with a roti (Indian pancake). A glass-walled kitchen means you can watch all the chefs in action.

Five Flies
14–16 Keerom Street; tel: 021 424 4442; www.fiveflies.co.za; $$; Mon–Fri noon–3pm, daily 7pm–late; map p.136 A2
Situated inside an elegant historic building with wood-panelled walls and an outdoor courtyard area. Always busy, it attracts lawyers from the nearby courts at lunchtime and a mixed bag of regulars in the evenings. The menu offers a modern take on classic cuisine using local produce and game cuts. Great winter specials.

Fork
84 Long Street; tel: 021 424 6334; www.fork-restaurants.

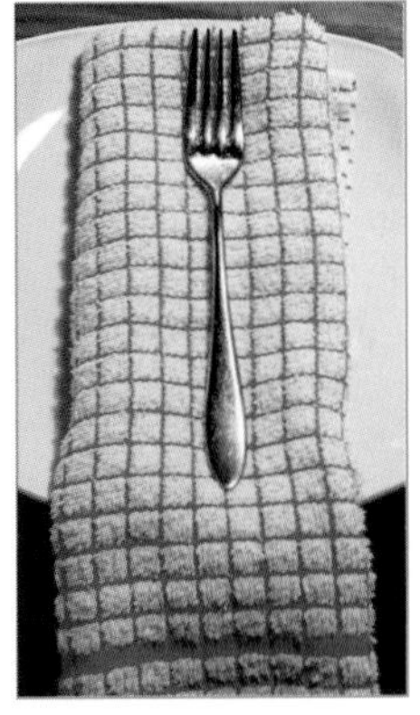

Left: Ginja.

co.za; $; Mon–Sat noon–11pm; map p.136 A2
Contemporary tapas-style food in a laid-back bistro setting. Situated on buzzing Long Street, step inside this industrial-style space with exposed brick walls, low-hanging lights and tea-towel napkins. Try the delicious tender lamb cutlets with cumin and coriander sauce, chorizo served with a cheese fondue or the diced tuna loin on a cannellini-bean salad. Excellent local wine list.

> Don't forget to try the street food and corner-shop offerings dotted around the City Centre. A must-try includes a samosa (triangle-shaped curried meat or vegetable pastry that is deep-fried) or a boerewors (farmer's sausage) roll with lashings of tomato sauce.

Ginja
121 Castle Street; tel: 021 426 2368; $$$; Mon–Sat 7–10.30pm; map p.136 A1
A moody restaurant that's consistently good. The food is delicious (start with a selection of tasting spoons of different world flavours) and then try the fusion-style pan-roasted ostrich. The wine list is extensive and the venue has a general bohemian feel attracting a sophisticated crowd. After dinner head upstairs to the venue's Shoga Bar for an Irish coffee.

Haiku
33 Church Street; tel: 021 424 7000; www.bukhara.com/haiku; $$$; Mon–Sat noon–3pm, daily 6pm–late; map p.136 A2
A Pan-Asian tapas venue in sexy surroundings. Think all-black interiors with low lighting and funky background music. The huge menu includes five-spice calamari, dim sum filled with spinach and cream cheese, teriyaki grills and their famous Peking duck. You'll find you have to eat quite a few dishes to be fully satisfied. Expect a hefty bill, but it's worth every cent.

Jardine
185 Bree Street; tel: 021 424 5640; www.jardineonbree.co.za; $$$; Mon–Sat noon–11pm; map p.136 A2
One of the city's most popular culinary destinations, offering an exceptional fine dining experience in a laid-back setting. Sit and watch chef George Jardine at work in his open-plan kitchen, preparing specials that include a beetroot tart, a famous lobster risotto or seared sirloin with Béarnaise sauce. Finish off with a shot of grappa. A new bakery next door serves warm bread and pastries during the day.

Masala Dosa Aromatic Cuisine
167 Long Street; tel: 021 424 6772; www.masaladosa.co.za; $; Mon–Sat 7.30am–10pm; map p.136 A3
A hip Indian restaurant on Long Street that's always crammed with people. Décor is plain and simple with white tables and chairs, and bright Bollywood posters cover the walls. Enjoy traditional Southern Indian dosa crêpes with your choice of fragrant curry fillings and spicy sambals. Their frozen berry lassi is the perfect ending to a colourful meal.

Nyoni's Kraal
98 Long Street; tel: 021 422 0529; www.nyoniskraal.co.za; $$; map p.136 A2
A traditional South African dining experience with hints of European flavours in funky surroundings. Try its signature pap and wors (sausage)

Prices for two-course meal per person with a half-bottle of house wine:
$ under R150
$$ R150–R200
$$$ R200–R300
$$$$ more than R300

towers made from steamed corn discs layered with tender steak, spinach, creamed butternut and whole-kernel sweetcorn and smothered in beef gravy. There's also marinated *snoek* and even mopani worms, an African delicacy, if you're feeling adventurous.

Royale Eatery

273 Long Street; tel: 021 422 4536; $; Mon–Sat noon–11.30pm; map p.136 A3

This is where the fashion pack come to refuel after a long day spent on movie sets and fashion shoots. Slip into one of the vinyl booths and be prepared to eat well. Gourmet burgers are the order of the day, and there's one for everyone whether it's beef, lamb, vegetarian or chicken with all the toppings and a mix of chips. Wash it all down with an icy Bar One milkshake for dessert.

City Bowl

Café Gainsbourg

64 Kloof Street; tel: 021 422 1780; $$; Mon–Fri 8am–10pm, Sat–Sun 9am–10.30pm; map p.135 E3

An airy bistro café that spills out onto the pavement with views up to the mountain. It's a low-key lunchtime hangout during the day, but at night it takes on a moody atmosphere, with sultry lighting and flickering candles. There's a small menu with pastas, salads and seafood that are simply prepared but

Right: Jardine.

Left and right: Willoughby & Co. for fresh seafood

big on flavour. The seared Norwegian salmon is a must-eat.

Cape Colony

Mount Nelson Hotel, 76 Orange Street, Gardens; tel: 021 483 1850; www.mountnelson hotel.co.za; $$$; daily 6.30–10.30pm; map p.135 E3

If you're looking for smart dining, executive chef Ian Mancais pulls out all the stops with his take on Asian meets African cuisine. The global glitterati, if they're in town, will be here too, dining under a huge mural depicting the city 200 years ago. Expect all-round top-notch service and a wine list featuring some notable Cape stars.

Chef Pon's Asian Kitchen

12 Mill Street, Gardens; tel: 021 465 5846; $; Mon–Sat 6–10.30pm; map p.136 A4

A favourite sit-down and take-out Asian eatery for city dwellers. All the best-known Asian dishes are on the menu, including a succulent crispy duck and tom yum soup. It is a busy and noisy venue, the wine is affordable, and the Asian beers are a welcome addition after a spoonful of the spicy red chicken curry.

Manna Epicure

Kloof Street, Gardens; tel: 021 426 2413; $–$$; Tue–Sat 9am–6pm, Sun 9am–4pm; map p.135 E4

A chic all-white interior crammed with beautiful people and exotic blooms. The food is fresh and imaginative, using the best of local ingredients. Breakfasts are sublime – the creamy scrambled eggs served with toasted coconut bread will keep you well satisfied for most of the day. There's always a cake table filled with treats, which also makes this a great venue for afternoon tea parties.

Nelson's Eye

9 Hof Street, Gardens; tel: 021 423 2601; $$; Tue–Fri noon–2pm, Sat–Sun 6.30pm–close; map p.135 E4

This is a typical old-school steakhouse, down to the wooden booths and wall-panelling. It's also one of the oldest grill houses in the city and continues to satisfy customers with its excellent steaks. Go for the kilogram T-bone steak if you're feeling ravenous, but its ladies fillet steak will also fill the gap. Great french fries and side orders of creamy spinach, onion rings and sweet pumpkin complement your meal.

> Some restaurants allow you to bring your own wine, although they may charge you a hefty corkage fee, so check beforehand. Often it works out more reasonable just to buy off their wine list.

Victoria and Alfred Waterfront

Belthazar Restaurant and Wine Bar

153 Victoria Basin; tel: 021 421 3753; www.belthazar.co.za; $$$; daily noon–11pm; map p.133 E4

People primarily come here to drink wine by the glass (there are around 100 to choose from). The food is simple but excellent: superb fillet, T-bone steaks and seafood. The shop next door sells chefs' knives, Riedel

Prices for two-course meal per person with a half bottle of house wine:
$ under R150
$$ R150–R200
$$$ R200–R300
$$$$ more than R300

glassware and T-shirts, as well as meat-to-go and sauces.

Beluga
The Foundry, Prestwich Street, Green Point; tel: 021 418 2948; www.beluga.co.za; $$; daily 10.30am–11.30pm; map p.133 D4
This is a busy, bistro-style restaurant for smart, young professionals who meet for lunch and light suppers after work. A large menu offers anything from steaks, ostrich and game to freshly caught fish and excellent sushi specials (during the week only). A varied and well-priced wine list.

one.waterfront
The Cape Grace Hotel, West Quay Road; tel: 021 418 0520; www.capegrace.com; $$$; daily 6.30am–10.30pm; map p.133 E3
Perfectly positioned with views of the yacht marina and Table Mountain, this is probably one of the nicest hotel dining rooms in the city. The décor, much like the new menu, is contemporary with a few easy-eating bistro additions like gourmet fish 'n' chips or fillet Béarnaise. After dinner visit the **Bascule** bar downstairs for a rare malt.
SEE ALSO BARS, P.33

The Showroom
1 Hospital Street, Harbour Edge, Green Point; tel: 021 421 4682; www.theshowroomrestaurant.co.za; $$–$$$; Tue–Fri noon–3pm, Mon–Sat 7–10.30pm; map p.133 E4
Owner and charismatic chef Bruce Robertson takes centre stage in his vibrant open plan kitchen. It's a good idea to book well in advance to experience a part of the action – you may not get a table otherwise. The menu is tongue-in-cheek and original; simply prepared seasonal ingredients with a list of sauces to match. A good wine selection with a few unusual bottles too.

Willoughby & Co.
Shop 6132, Lower Level, Victoria Wharf, V&A Waterfront; tel: 021 418 6116; $–$$; daily 11am–11pm; map p.133 E2
Newly revamped and re-opened, Willoughby's may be situated deep inside the V&A's main shopping centre, with no ocean views, but it does keep serious sushi afi-

cionados coming back for more. There's also a wide range of wok-style dishes, calamari and a classic line fish grilled and served to you in a cast-iron pan. You can't book, so just turn up and wait your turn. Also sells deli items and wet fish.

Bo-Kaap

Biesmiellah

Corner of Wale and Pentz streets; tel: 021 423 0850; $; Mon–Sat 8.30am–10.30pm; map p.136 A2

This restaurant is a must. In fact it's a private house, and you come here to eat well-prepared and authentic Cape Malay cooking. This is where they serve some of the best home-made breyanis in the city. No alcohol.

Noon Gun Tearoom

273 Longmarket Street; tel: 021 424 0529; $; Mon–Sat 10am–9pm, during fasting months 10am–5pm; map p.136 A2

A popular midday stop for tourists exploring the city centre. Specialising in Cape Malay cooking, the Noon Gun Tearoom at the top of Longmarket Street serves set lunches and dinners and teas. No alcohol.

Southern Suburbs

The Hussar Grill

10 Main Road, Rondebosch; tel: 021 689 9516; www.hussargrill.com; $$; Mon–Fri noon–11pm, Sat 6–11pm, Sun noon–10pm

This restaurant has been around for more than 40 years and continues to serve some of the best rump steak in town. However, the Madagascan pepper fillet is equally good. The menu also covers some game dishes if you're a serious carnivore. Enjoy a decent bottle of red wine with your dish of choice.

> Call in at Atlas Trading Company at 94 Wale Street in Bo-Kaap, opposite the museum, and buy some of the herbs or spices used in Cape Malay food. The owners will happily share recipes and cooking tips with you.

Myoga

Vineyard Hotel, 60 Colinton Road, Newlands; tel: 021 657 4545; www.vineyard.co.za; $$$; Mon–Sat 11am–2pm; 7–10pm

This hotel restaurant has been recently transformed into another successful creation under the ownership of chef and entrepreneur Mike Bassett (of Ginja restaurant fame, *see p.104*). Housed in an early Cape farmhouse but vibrantly updated with bright-orange sofas and black crystal chandeliers, Bassett serves swanky global fusion cuisine paired with an impressively varied wine list. Expect to find a long meze-style table over lunch offering platters of Eastern and Mediterranean flavours. You can also just enjoy a drink in the gardens facing the eastern flank of Table Mountain.

Wijnhuis

Corner of Kildare Road and Main Street, Newlands; tel: 021 671 9705; www.wijnhuis.co.za; $$; Mon–Sat 8am–11pm

As you would expect of somewhere called Wijnhuis (wine house), it offers a list of specialised wines to go with good, modern Italian food like simple meat dishes, pasta and pizza. The lofty interior offers a relaxed atmosphere with comfy sofas for post-dining lounging. The waiters can be a bit stiff, but the food makes up for it.

Constantia Valley and Kirstenbosch

Buitenverwachting

Klein Constantia Road, Constantia; tel: 021 794 5190; www.buitenverwachting.co.za; $$$; Easter–Oct: Tue–Sat noon–2pm, 6.30–10pm, Nov–Easter: Mon–Sat noon–3pm, 6.30–10pm

The food at Buitenverwachting is classic country cuisine (foie gras, pan-fried Norwegian salmon, rack of lamb, etc) with contemporary influences and some local twists. It's rather pricey, but it's situated in a typical Cape Dutch homestead, with lovely views of the vineyards. The menu changes regularly, using only the finest seasonal ingredients.

The Cape Malay Restaurant

The Cellars-Hohenort Hotel, 93 Brommersvlei Road, Constantia; tel: 021 794 2137; www.collectionmcgrath.com; $$$; Tue–Sat 7–9.30pm

This is one of the grandest hotels in the Southern Suburbs, occupying an old private mansion set in a magnificent garden in the heart of Constantia. The authentic Malay-oriented food gives you a glimpse into South Africa's food heritage. There's also an extensive wine list.

Catharina's Restaurant

Steenberg Hotel, Steenberg Estate, Tokai Road, Constantia; tel: 021 713 2222; www.steenberghotel.com; $$$; daily breakfast 7–10.30am, noon–3pm, 7–10pm

Come here for a close-up view of Steenberg, the oldest farm in the Constantia Valley. The new-look interior comes with a simplified menu that changes weekly. Expect generous and hearty dishes presented with great care. Enjoy a drink under the old oaks out at the front before dinner. Alternatively there's a lighter lunch menu, and sundowners and tapas are served by the sexy poolside bar.

Prices for two-course meal per person with a half-bottle of house wine:
$ under R150
$$ R150–R200
$$$ R200–R300
$$$$ more than R300

Jonkershuis
Groot Constantia Estate, Groot Constantia Road, Constantia; tel: 021 794 6255; www.jonkershuisconstantia.co.za; $$; Mon–Sat 9am–10pm, Sun 9am–5pm
The renovated interior to this Cape Dutch farmhouse is an ideal setting for family lunches (an extremely child-friendly venue), serving hearty French-style dishes and a few Cape Malay specialities. It has a wine bar, deli and shady courtyard, creating a strong country bistro feel.

La Colombe
Constantia Uitsig Wine Estate, Spaanschemat River Road, Constantia; tel: 021 794 2390; www.constantia-uitsig.com; $$$; Mon–Sat 12.30–2.30pm, 7.30–9.30pm
This is another Constantia Valley great. Chef-of-the-moment Luke Dale-Roberts is taking charge with his bold flavours, creative textures and impressive presentation. The menu leans towards French country cooking with a blackboard menu written up in French and ably explained by the well-trained waiting staff. The décor, like that at the Constantia Uitsig Hotel *(see p.65)*, is un-pretentious and simple.

Uitsig Restaurant
Constantia Uitsig Wine Estate, Spaanschemat River Road, Constantia; tel: 021 794 4480; www.constantia-uitsig.com; $$$; 12.30–2.30pm, 7.30–9.30pm

Right: Jonkershuis in Constantia.

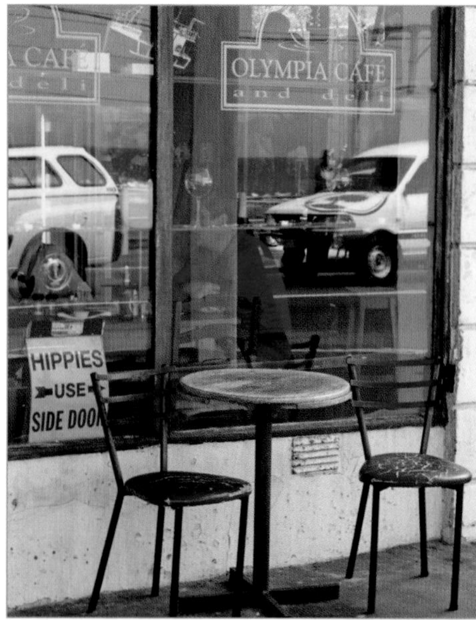

Left: Olympia Café and Deli in Kalk Bay.

One of the city's best places to eat, set in the heart of the Constantia Uitsig vineyards. The Italian-inspired cuisine like the featherlight pastas and superb tagliata along with Uitsig's delicious wines, brings people back time and time again.

Atlantic Seaboard and Cape Peninsula

ATLANTIC SEABOARD

Café Neo
129 Beach Road, Mouille Point; tel: 021 433 0849; $; daily 7am–7pm; map p.132 B2
This is a trendy little hot spot with great sea views and a big outdoor wooden deck, ideal for lazy breakfasts and lunches. There's a large chalkboard menu inside featuring an all-day Greek breakfast, salads, tapas and gourmet sandwiches.

Geisha Wok and Noodle Bar
Surrey Place, Mouille Point; tel: 021 439 0533; www.geisha-wokandnoodlebar.com; Mon–Sat noon–11pm, Sun noon–10.30pm; map p.132 C2
A unique style of Asian tapas, with over 30 wok and noodle dishes. An all-white sexy interior, which can be a bit on the bright side at night, but it pulls in a sophisticated, young crowd. Favourites on the menu worth tasting are the spicy prawn dim sum and the wok-fried sliced duck breast for something a little more filling. For non-drinkers, they serve freshly squeezed juices, or there's a cheeky cocktail menu for the adventurous types.

La Perla
Beach Road, Sea Point; tel: 021 434 2471; $$; daily 11am–11pm; map p.134 B1
The most famous restaurant on the Atlantic Seaboard, which recently underwent a major revamp for the first time in 50 years. La Perla is always busy, especially over high season, so be sure to book. Good fish, meat and poultry, pasta, massive salads and sorbets. A neighbourhood haunt where swanky locals let their hair down.

Newport Market and Deli
47 Beach Road, Mouille Point; tel: 021 439 1538; $; daily 7.30am–8pm; map p.132 C2
This popular deli and café is jam-packed over weekends with families, cyclists, promenade joggers and socialites, especially for early breakfasts and brunch (sadly no greasy fry-ups, only healthy mueslis, smoothies and bagels). For lunch or light suppers there are wraps, salads and soups. A great spot to read the weekend newspapers in the afternoon sun.

Posticino
3 Albany Mews, 323 Main Road, Sea Point; tel: 021 439 4014; $; daily noon–11pm; map p.132 A4
This bustling pizzeria offers a warm welcome, and has a vibrant pavement area where most people gather on warmer summer evenings. It serves some of the best pizza and pasta in town, where you can mix and match your toppings. They also have a well-priced wine list.

Salt
Ambassador Hotel, Victoria Road, Bantry Bay; tel: 021 439 7258; www.saltrestaurant.co.za; $$$; daily 12.30–10.30pm; map p.134 A3
This is possibly the best seat on the Atlantic Seaboard for

> A typical South African dessert is a Malva pudding – a caramel-toffee flavoured pudding served warm with custard or cream.

Right: enjoy fresh sushi at Wakame in Mouille Point.

its spectacular views (you're basically suspended over the ocean) and for the bistro-type food. A small but well-chosen menu of modern international dishes and tapas. Decadent desserts and very affordable local wines (over 70 to choose from), that you can enjoy by the glass too.

The Sandbar
31 Victoria Road, Camps Bay; tel: 021 438 8336; www.sandbar.co.za; $; daily 9.30am–11pm; map p.138 A3
A buzzing beachfront café that was recently revamped into a chic beach bar, where you can still sit with sand on your toes after a long day on the beach. A snacky meze and tapas menu for those feeling peckish and other more substantial items like gourmet sandwiches and wraps. A great spot for brunch when the weather is good.

Wakame
Corner of Beach Road and Surrey Place, Mouille Point; tel: 021 433 2377; www.wakame.co.za; $$; Mon–Thur noon–3pm, 6–10.30pm, Fri–Sat noon–3.30pm, 6–11pm, Sun 6–10.30am; map p.132 C2
This is a busy seaside restaurant and sushi bar, with one of the best ocean views in town. Expect Pacific Rim food with Asian-style dishes and a sprinkling of classic European and American fare (the sweet and salty calamari is out of this world). There's also a good sushi bar for those wanting something a little lighter. It attracts a fashionable crowd, sometimes just for a drink.

CAPE PENINSULA

Chapman's Restaurant
Chapman's Peak Hotel, Chapman's Peak Drive; tel: 021 790 1036; $; daily noon–10pm
Chapman's is a very popular hotel restaurant with a good seafood menu. It is most famous for its deep-fried calamari, fries and seaside views. Also good for weekend lunches if you want to linger for hours on the covered terrace overlooking the bay.

Harbour House
Kalk Bay Harbour; tel: 021 788 4133; www.harbourhouse.co.za; $$; daily noon–4pm, 6–10pm
This popular harbourside restaurant with its simply stylish interiors offers excellent and inexpensive dining with panoramic ocean views. Freshly caught fish is imaginatively prepared (try the chermoula prawns) with good salads and great wines.

The Foodbarn
Noordhoek Farm Village, Village Lane, Noordhoek; tel: 021 789 1390; www.thefoodbarn.co.za; $; daily 8am–5pm, Wed–Fri only
Award-winning former La Colombe chef Franck Dangereux gets it right at his new modest farm venue. Enjoy a typically French breakfast of pastries and coffee, Japanese-style tuna tartare or a hearty meal like polenta gnocchi for early dinner with your children. Good value for money too.

Kitima
Kronendal Estate, 140 Main Road, Hout Bay; tel: 021 790-8004; www.kitima.co.za; Mon noon–3pm, Sun, Tue–Sat noon–3pm, 5.30–11.30pm
Located in the old Kronendal Homestead, this is a hidden gem in the Hout Bay Valley. An Asian line-up of dishes like dim sum, sushi and satays are perfect for sharing, followed by popular wok-fry dishes and other steamed delicacies. Reservations are essential.

Olympia Café and Deli
134 Main Road, Kalk Bay; tel: 021 788 6396; $–$$; daily 7am–9pm

Prices for two-course meal per person with a half-bottle of house wine:
$ under R150
$$ R150–R200
$$$ R200–R300
$$$$ more than R300

Really great food in a bohemian atmosphere – this is the queen of Cape cafés. For brunch, take the papers, order a jug of coffee and settle down with poached eggs and smoked salmon. Everything here from the shellfish to the cakes is first-class. Due to it's popularity, its usually mayhem trying to get a table over the weekend, so get there early. A bakery next door sells the best ciabatta in town.

Cape Winelands

Bouillabaisse
38 Huguenot Road, Franschhoek; tel: 021 876 4430; www.seafooddeli.co.za; $$; Mon–Sat 10am–10pm

This is a contemporary champagne-meets-oyster bar with sexy interiors and a seafood tapas-style menu. It's rather cramped for space, but perfect for a quick, light meal. The focus is on seafood tasters at set prices that are small mouthfuls but very flavoursome. Try the fish wontons, scallops, and of course their signature bouillabaisse.

Bread & Wine
Moreson Winery, Happy Valley Road, La Motte, Franschhoek; tel: 021 876 3692; www.moreson.co.za; $$$; Tue–Sun noon–3pm

An authentic country restaurant idyllically set among the estate's vineyards and orchards, Bread & Wine is a great place to stop for lunch. It has a courtyard and covered terrace, and a Mediterranean-inspired menu featuring a good range of meat and seafood, homemade sausages, pastas, etc. Freshly prepared dishes are made with top-quality ingredients. The freshly baked breads dunked into bowls of olive oil are just one reason to go back for more.

Right: La Petite Ferme in Franschhoek.

Left and below left: Bouillabaisse serves light, tasty seafood.

The Goatshed

Fairview Wine Farm, Suid Agter Paarl; tel: 021 863 3609; www.fairview.co.za; $–$$; daily 9am–5pm

A charming barn-style restaurant decorated with a huge image of a goatherd on the wall. Choose from a variety of cheese and meat platters and daily chalkboard specials, accompanied by carafes of the estate's wine. It's well worth a drive out into the country and welcomes children of all ages.

La Petite Ferme

North of town on the Franschhoek Pass Road, Franschhoek; tel: 021 876 3016; www.lapetitferme.co.za; $$$; daily noon–4pm

Here you can enjoy a hearty meal or mid-afternoon coffee and cakes on an attractive terrace overlooking the Franschhoek Valley. Try the slow-roasted lamb with minted yoghurt sauce and spicy pommes frites or the balti butter chicken curry.

The Tasting Room

Le Quartier Français, 16 Huguenot Street, Franschhoek; tel: 021 876 2151; www.lequartier.co.za; $$$$; daily 7pm to late

An award-winning restaurant under the helm of wonder chef Margot Janse, featuring four-, six- and eight-course tasting menus served with meticulously selected Cape wines. Its cooking reflects the influence of the region's original French settlers. For something a little more

> Prices for two-course meal per person with a half bottle of house wine:
> $ under R150
> $$ R150–R200
> $$$ R200–R300
> $$$$ more than R300

Left: The Tasting Room.
Below: 34 South.

casual, the adjoining iCi bistro and bar serves classy and affordable pub grub.

Terroir

Kleine Zalze Wine Farm, off R44, Stellenbosch; tel: 021 880 8167; www.kleinezalze.com; $$; Mon–Sun noon–2pm, Mon–Sat 6.45–9.30pm

An earthy farmhouse restaurant, with terracotta floor tiles and crisp white linen tablecloths. Chef Michael Broughton's ever-changing menu celebrates seasonal, locally sourced ingredients, elegantly presented and delicious to eat. An emphasis is placed on matching the food to specific wines produced on the Kleine Zalze estate. All-round excellent quality. Booking is essential.

Tokara

Hellshoogte Pass, Stellenbosch; tel: 021 808 5959; www.tokara.co.za; $$$; Tue–Sat noon–3pm, 7pm until late

Set in a beautiful space overlooking rolling vineyards and mountains; get ready for a gastronomic feast of flavours in the form of sauces, stocks and reductions served with the finest-quality fish and meat. This is a must-try venue for all serious foodies taking a trip through the Winelands.

Overberg

Seafood at The Marine

The Marine Hermanus, Marine Drive, Hermanus; tel: 028 313 1000; www.collectionmcgrath.com; $$$; daily noon–2pm, 7–9pm

A luxury hotel dining room with a fresh, modern appeal. Set inside a casual and comfortable setting with high-quality fare, its small menu focuses on fish and seafood – the 'rich man's fish and chips' is superb. Prices are high.

Garden Route

GEORGE

Margot's Bistro

63 Albert Street, George; tel: 044 874 2950; $; Tue 8.30am–5pm,

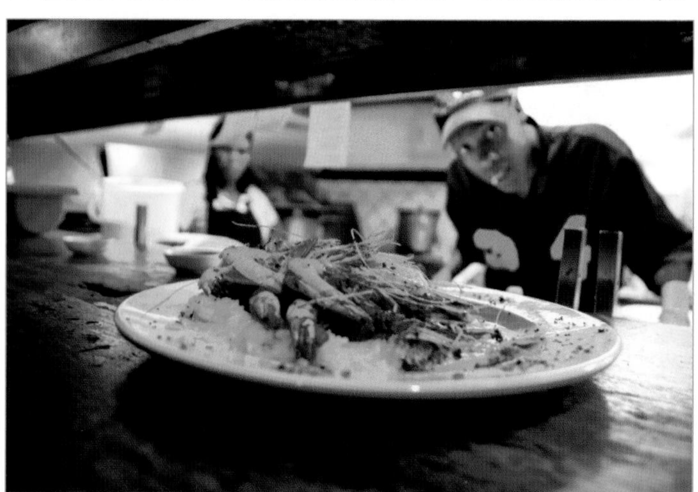

Prices for two-course meal per person with a half bottle of house wine:
$ under R150
$$ R150–R200
$$$ R200–R300
$$$$ more than R300

Wed–Sat 8.30am–5pm, 7pm to late
A stylishly converted house with swish interiors. A small yet efficient kitchen that delivers bistro-style food during the day and more sophisticated dishes in the evening. Try the saffron-poached pears stuffed with gorgonzola and wrapped in pancetta – a heavenly delight.

KNYSNA

34 South
Knysna Quays, Waterfront Drive, Knysna; tel: 044 382 7268; www.34-south.com; $$; daily 8.30am–10pm
Pleasantly laid-back and very popular with visitors. Sit out on the deck and order platters of oysters, sardines, freshly grilled line-fish or seafood paella. Good wine selection too.

Cornuti Al Mar Restaurant and Bar
1 Perestrella Street, Plettenberg Bay; tel: 044 533 1277; $$; daily noon–11pm
This is the place to be and be seen over the busy festive season in December. Light and airy with a great balcony, the thin-based pizzas are crisp and perfect. The homemade pastas are scrumptious too. Head over to the trendy bar for a cocktail after your meal.

Left: enjoy oysters in Knysna

Il de Pain Bread & Café
10 The Boatshed, Thesen Harbour Town; tel: 044 302 5707; $–$$; Tue–Fri 7am–5pm, Sat 7am–3pm, Sun 9am–1.30pm
This is where you stop for the best freshly baked, hand-crafted sourdough breads and pastries on the Garden Route, thanks to the wood-fired oven and stone-ground flour kneaded with wild yeast. Locals sip coffee and munch on croissants, quiches and sandwiches layered with local cheeses, meats and home-made relishes.

Knysna Oyster Company
Thesen Island, Knysna Quays; tel: 044 382 6942; www.knysnaoysters.co.za; $$; winter: daily 10am–7pm, summer: daily 9am–9pm
Established in 1949, the Knysna Oyster Company is renowned for its oysters, cultivated in the Knysna River estuary close by. Situated on the lagoon, this venue is great for waterside sundowners (oysters with champagne) as well as seafood, grills and game meals.

Shopping

While sightseeing in and around Cape Town is essential, spending some time in the shops, markets and malls is also a not-to-be-missed experience. Whether you're looking for stylish décor and design, local art and craft or something special to wear, you're sure to find it. This is a city guaranteed to give you a satisfying dose of retail therapy. For further shopping opportunities *see also Fashion, p.50–1,* for clothing stores for men and women; *Food and Drink, p.56–7,* for specialist food stores; *Markets, Streets and Squares, p.74–5,* for alfresco finds; and *Pampering, p.95,* for smellies.

African Arts, Crafts and Curios

Cape Town is a Mecca for traders from all over Africa. At **Greenmarket Square** on Shortmarket Street in the City Centre you'll find a huge range of goods including jewels, tribal masks, wooden sculpture, beadwork and handmade clothing. An excellent lightweight gift is one of the locally produced wire sculptures that are sold by the roadside, ranging from wire flowers to a life-sized wire lion.

SEE ALSO MARKETS, STREETS AND SQUARES, P.75

Africa Nova

Cape Quarter, 72 Waterkant Street, De Waterkant; tel: 021 425 5123; www.africanova.co.za; Mon–Fri 10am–5pm, Sat 10am–3pm; map p.136 A1

Africa Nova is a high-end boutique shop offering beautifully crafted ceramics, intricately beaded jewellery and other decorative objects.

Montebello Design Centre

31 Newlands Avenue, Newlands; tel: 021 685 6445; www.montebello.co.za; Mon–Fri 9am–5pm, Sat 9am–3.30pm, Sun 9am–3pm

For ethnic crafts, this is a great choice.

Antiques

Antique-lovers should take a leisurely stroll down **Church Street**, a short road off Long Street that's an arcade of antiques and bookshops, where you are guaranteed to find a real bargain. If you're blessed with a magpie's eye, then **Kalk Bay** with its quirky antique and collectable shops is a must for all trawlers on the hunt for something special.

Burr & Muir

82 Church Street, City Centre; tel: 021 422 1319; www.burrmuir.spinner.co.za; Mon–Fri 9.30am–4.30pm, Sat 9.30am–1pm; map p.136 A2

Burr & Murr mostly specialises in glassware and ceramics from the Art Deco and Art Nouveau periods.

Private Collections

66 Waterkant Street; tel: 021 421 0298; Mon–Fri 8am–5pm, Sat 8am–2.30pm; map p.136 A1

In the trendy design quarter of De Waterkant, this is a good place to look for Anglo-

Left: tribal masks for sale at Greenmarket Square.
Right: bric-a-brac at Kalk Bay.

Left: designer shopping at Victoria Wharf.

> Whether you choose to buy your craft from the side of the road or from a designer inner-city store, take the time to find out about the people who have produced the product and what's helped them make it a truly South African piece.

Raj antiques, including 19th-century Indian architectural antiques and furniture.

Electronics

Audiovision
Shop 6124, Lower Level, V&A Waterfront; tel: 021 421 1055; www.audiovision.co.za; daily 9am–9pm; map p.133 E2
For those wanting a technology upgrade, try here for the latest in digital cameras. They also stock other audiovisual equipment such as state-of-the-art surround sound, DVD players, etc.

Incredible Connection
Shop 5 E&S Building, Lower Loop Street, City Centre; tel: 021 441 2420; www.incredible.co.za; Mon–Fri 9am–5.30pm, Sat 9am–2pm, Sun 10am–1pm; map p.136 B1
If you're in the business for computers and electronic gadgets, head to Incredible Connections, an over-the-top store that's always stocked with the latest and greatest laptops and other digital things.

Floral Design

For something blooming gorgeous for either yourself or someone special, try these city florists for a memorable creation.

Aspen
113 Long Street, City Centre; tel: 021 424 6511; www.aspenflowers.co.za; Mon–Fri 8am–4.30pm; map p.136 A2
For fresh flowers with a twist, this charming flower shop has everything from that take-away bunch to over-the-top installations.

Lush
13A Kloof Nek Road, Gardens; tel: 021 423 5503; Mon–Fri 9.30am–4pm; map p.135 E3
This is where you come if you're looking for something unusual yet beautiful. A popular choice amongst edgy brides to be.

Home Décor

Cape Town is a hotbed of local design talent when it comes to homeware.

Imagenius
117 Long Street, City Centre; tel: 021 423 7870;

Left: crafted croc.

www.imagenius.co.za; Mon–Fri 9.30am–4.30am, Sat 9.30am–1.30pm; map p.136 A2
Try Imagenius for something quirky with a strong African flavour.

Lim
86A Kloof Street, Gardens; tel: 021 423 1200; www.lim.co.za; Mon–Fri 9am–5pm, Sat 9.15am–1pm; map p.135 E3
For special hand-picked pieces with an organic feel, try Lim. Here you'll find mostly locally produced and hand-crafted products with a modern edge.

L'Orangerie
7 Wolfe Street, Wynberg; tel: 021 761 8355; Mon–Fri 9am–5pm, Sat 9.30am–1.30pm
If you're looking for vintage French linen, crystal glassware and jars of gorgeous-smelling things, this is the place to visit.

Okha
109 Hatfield Street, Gardens; tel: 021 461 7233; www.okha.com; Mon–Fri 8.30am–5pm, Sat 9am–1pm; map p.136 A3
Okha is a sexy design studio and showroom featuring customised contemporary furnishings and accessories. Glass tables, structural lighting and ceramic vessels to die for.

Jewellery and Accessories

Bead Boys
Old Biscuit Mill, 373 Albert Road, Woodstock; tel: 021 448 4499; www.beadmerchantsofafrica.com; Mon–Fri 9am–4.45pm, Sat 9am–4pm
This shop has the most colourful bead collections, separated into gorgeous colour-coordinated displays in every shape, length and size. Either make up your own string with the beads available or pick one ready-made from their enormous collection.

Charles Greig
Shop U6224, Victoria Wharf, V&A Waterfront; tel: 021 418 4515; www.charlesgreig.com; daily 9am–9pm; map p.133 E2
For diamonds, watches, bling and on-trend creations, this is one of the most sophisticated jewellery stores in town. It's also the official Rolex retailer in the country.

Occhiali Shop
135 Victoria Wharf; tel: 021 418 2825; daily 9am–9pm; map p.133 E2
Big-name brand sunglasses and prescription spectacles in line with international trends and labels. Also the place for hot-off-the-catwalk designs.

Olive Green Cat
1st Floor, 51 Wale Street, City Centre; tel: 021 424 1101;

Right: ostrich-egg lamps and other crafts at the V&A Waterfront.

Mon–Fri 8am–5pm, Sat by appointment only; map p.136 A2
Two of South Africa's most talented contemporary jewellery designers sell their pieces at this studio store. Think perspex engraved cuffs with diamonds, etched rings and other innovative accessories.

Tanzanite International
Shop 118, Clock Tower Precinct, V&A Waterfront; tel: 021 421 5488; www.tanzanite-int.com; Mon–Sat 9am–8.30pm, Sat 10am–8.30pm; map p.133 E3
Tanzanite is one of the most sought-after precious stones in the world, and this specialist is where you'll find that special brilliant-blue rock you'll pass down to generations to come.

Shopping Centres

Canal Walk
Century Boulevard, Century City; tel: 021 555 4444; www.canalwalk.co.za; daily 9am–9pm
This is the place to be if you are in serious shopping mood. Just be prepared for the crowds, especially over weekends, and the long walk around over 100 stores in the centre. There is an enormous food court and a large cinema complex for post-shopping entertainment.

For décor and furniture head to the Cape Quarter 72 Waterkant Street, De Waterkant, tel: 021 421 0737; www.capequarter.co.za. Here you'll find everything from Indian architectural pieces to a myriad of handmade African jewellery, decorative ceramics and designer sunglasses.

Cavendish Square
1 Dreyer Street, Claremont; tel: 021 657 5600; www.cavendish.co.za; Mon–Sat 9am–7pm, Sun 10am–5pm
A stylish shopping haven in the heart of the Southern Suburbs with everything from music stores to jewellery franchises, retail fashion outlets and restaurants.

Gardens Centre
Mill Street, Gardens; tel: 021 465 1842; www.gardenshoppingcentre.co.za; Mon–Fri 9am–7pm, Sat 9am–5pm, Sun 9am–2pm; map p.136 A4
This is a local shopping mall which is best for grocery shopping but also home to a number of boutique shops, gift shops, homeware finds, and hardware stores. You can also get a light lunch at one of the daytime restaurants on site.

Portside
1 Upper Portswood Road, Green Point; tel: 021 419 0440; daily 9am–6pm; map p.133 D3
Independent retailers, fabric showrooms, shoe shops, boutique clothing and contemporary furniture. A great meeting spot for early-morning coffee and people-watching.

Victoria Wharf
V&A Waterfront; tel: 021 408 7600; www.waterfront.co.za; Mon–Sat 9am–9pm, Sun 10am–9pm; map p.133 E2
Clothing chain stores, movie houses, pharmacies, international fashion brands and curio boutiques. This is a one-stop shop for shopping, eating and entertainment. Be prepared for the crowds over the festive season. And try to book for movies and restaurants in advance.

Sport

South Africans are mad about sport, and none more so than Capetonians. From extreme sports such as paragliding, shark-cage diving and spelunking (that's caving to the layman) to the more leisurely – though no less competitive – options of cricket, rugby and football, the city's well-positioned stadiums are packed all year round and the natural resources are there to be jumped off, dived into and surfed. Take care if you decide to go jogging or mountain-biking alone, as there are some unfortunate sporting activities, better-known as muggings, that usually occur on quieter parts of the city's mountainside.

Stadiums

Green Point Stadium

Granger Bay Boulevard, Green Point, V&A Waterfront; for details visit www.capetown.gov.za; map p.133 C3

Situated about two decent goal kicks from the ocean in Green Point, the construction of this 70,000-seater football stadium caused a lot of controversy in Cape Town. Many Green Point residents opposed it, listing the loss of greenery, traffic congestion and the availability of more appropriate locations for a mega-stadium. Logistically it never made sense, as the selected site is difficult for tens of thousands of people to access.

Nevertheless, the setting is undeniably beautiful and construction went ahead. Once completed, this will be one of the most beautiful stadiums in the world.

A few hours from Cape Town is the Karoo town of Oudtshoorn, famous for its ostrich farms and the **Cango Caves**, a massive underground labyrinth of limestone caves, dripstone caverns and stalactites. For some extreme fun, go spelunking on either an easy or advanced tour (not recommended for pregnant travellers or anyone suffering from claustrophobia). Daily except Christmas, every hour on the hour. Tel: 044 272 7410; www.cangocaves.co.za.

Newlands Rugby Stadium

11 Boundary Road, Newlands; tel: 021 659 4600; www.wprugby.com; entrance charge

The home of the provincial team, Western Province, and the region's Super 14 team, the Stormers, Newlands rugby stadium is one of South Africa's most famous rugby fortresses. Get invited to one of the hospitality suites, or rough it in the standing section of the Railway Stand, where you will experience some of the finest *vloeking* (swearing) ever thrown at a referee.

Sahara Park

Newlands Cricket Ground, Newlands; tel: 021 657 2003; www.capecobras.co.za; entrance charge

South Africa's colonial legacy is evident in the architecture, languages and surnames you'll find that indicate the presence of European visitors over the centuries. Something else that's stayed behind is British sports such as cricket,

Left: paragliding off the coast of Garden Route.

A big wave-surfing competition held off the Cape Peninsula coast near Hout Bay, the **Red Bull Big Wave Africa** runs between 24 July and 31 August each year, when huge winter swells batter the coast and break over a reef at a spot called Dungeons. Surfers face severe injury or death if they wipe out on waves that measure at least 4.5–6 metres (15–20ft). Fortunately, spectators can watch the daredevils from the coast. *See* www.redbullbwa.com.

Left: a cricket match in Outdshoorn.

rugby and football. One of the best ways to spend a weekend during summer in Cape Town is get a ticket in the Oaks section of Newlands Cricket Ground (currently called Sahara Park) and relax in the shade with a beer while visiting teams try to outstrategise the South African national team, the Proteas, in a five-day test. Newlands is also home to the provincial cricket side, the Cape Cobras.

Cycling

Cape Town hosts three of South Africa's biggest cycling events in the form of the **Giro del Capo** (www.girodelcapo.co.za), the **Cape Epic** (www.cape-epic.com) and the **Cape Argus Pick 'n' Pay Cycle Tour** (www.cycletour.co.za). The Argus takes place in March every year, with around 40,000 riders taking part in the event. For information visit www.bicycling.co.za.

Right: cycling the Franschhoek Pass.

Golf

Cape Town is filled with lush, green and well-manicured golf courses with fancy clubhouses. Whilst green fees can be quite pricey, caddies are relatively cheap, and daily rates change according to the season.

Mowbray Golf Course
Raapenberg Road, Mowbray, Cape Town; tel: 021 685 3018; www.mowbraygolfclub.co.za

Paragliding

Cape Town is a spectacular spot to go airborne. Try paragliding off Lion's Head, high above the beach bums on Camps Bay or Clifton's beaches.

Birdmen Paragliding
tel: 021 557 8144/082 658 6710; www.birdmen.co.za

Shark Diving

The Western Cape is home to a healthy population of huge Great white sharks (Carcharodon carcharias). The best way to get to see them up close and personal is through the bars of a cage. Shark-cage diving off Gansbaai, while controversial, is undoubtedly the most fun you'll have near a shark. For details contact tel:028 312 4293; or visit www.greatwhitesharkdiving.co.za

Townships

Most visitors get their first glimpse of the city's townships on their drive from the airport on the busy N2 highway as it sweeps into the city from the Southern Cape, crossing the infamous Cape Flats. These windy and dusty flatlands, prone to flooding, that lie between the wealthy Southern Suburbs and the Hottentots Holland Mountains, are also where the majority of Cape Town's population live. A half-day tour through the townships comes highly recommended and will introduce you to the African culture, community life and history, while you meet the local township people.

History

The townships include Langa (Sun), Gugulethu (Our Pride), Nyanga (Moon), Khayelitsha (New Place), Crossroads, Bonteheuwel, Hanover Park (named after District Six's main street) and Bishop Lavis Town. They are the areas in which non-whites were forced to live during the Apartheid years. Blacks, 'Coloureds' and Indians were separated into their own areas.

Several of the black townships have evolved from what were essentially labour camps, where male-only hostels for migrant workers from the Transkei and elsewhere were set up to meet the needs of the nearby city.

Townships Today

Mostly for economic reasons, people continue to live in the townships in which they were born. But the inhabitants also stay for social reasons. Extensive communities of families and friends have evolved, many of whom have lived together for nearly half a century. However, many non-white Capetonians have started moving into white suburbs. Since the new government came into power in 1994, the townships have improved dramatically with basic services such as electricity and water.

Despite this, crime and violence are still evident today. It is therefore highly inadvisable for strangers to enter a township independently. Roads are also badly signposted and maintained.

Township Tours

The only safe way to visit a township is to join an organised tour with people who know the locals and know precisely where to go. A trip to a township offers the chance to experience a living

Visitors are encouraged to support local artists and community projects by buying produce and merchandise on sale. They can even spend a night in a township. Conditions will be simple, and almost certainly mean sharing a bathroom with a stranger, but this is about looking at the way township people do things and, more importantly, it's about joining them. It is a relevant cultural exchange with people who rarely get the chance to meet foreigners.

Left: makeshift homes on the Meiringspoort Pass.

culture – to meet the locals in township taverns, jazz clubs and restaurants and browse among roadside stalls or chat to street vendors. Most tours visit the craft centres, a local *shebeen* (traditional drinking house), churches and an 'informal' home. For more information and bookings contact **Grassroots**, tel: 021 706 1006, or **Legend Tours**, tel: 021 697 4056.

If you're keen to hang out at a cool venue in the townships head for Mzoli's Place, 150 NY 111, Gugulethu; tel: 021 638 1355; daily 9am–6pm. This is where locals gather for a festive consumption of meat and beer. A cosmopolitan hot spot for politicians, celebs and white South Africans wanting a taste of the townships.

Langa

Langa, a few kilometres east of Mowbray, is currently being transformed into a modern suburb complete with schools, clinics and sports facilities. The Church was, and remains, an important institution which helped keep society together. Langa is one of the more organised and suburban townships, with homes of bricks and mortar.

Gugulethu

A tour of Gugulethu 2, 20km (12 miles) southeast of Cape Town, is likely to include visits to several struggle sites, where important and often tragic events during the fight against Apartheid are commemorated. Also on the itinerary will be the Sivuyile Tourism Centre, which caters for about 80 artists, making pottery and painting fabrics.

Khayelitsha

The second-largest township in South Africa (after Soweto near Johannesburg) which covers about 28sq km (11sq miles) 35km (22 miles) east of Cape Town along the N2 to Somerset West. There's a mix of formal and informal dwellings, the latter constantly growing as more people flow in from the countryside.

A visit to Khayelitsha normally begins with an overview of the township from Lookout Hill. It will also include the Khayelitsha Craft Market, set up in 1997 as a self-help organisation.

Lwandle Migrant Labour Museum

Old Community Hall, Vulindlela Street; tel: 021 845 6119; Mon–Fri 9.30am–4pm; entrance charge

Further along the N2 from Khayelitsha, towards Strand on the False Bay Coast, is the Lwandle Migrant Labour Museum. Housed in a former hostel, it preserves life as it was for the migrant labourers and documents the rules by which they lived.

Right and above left: residents of a township near Knysna.

Transport

This chapter gives you the low-down on how to get to Cape Town and how to get around the city once you arrive. There is really no need to get lost in Cape Town, thanks to the giant mountain as a landmark. However, getting lost on foot is probably the best way to get to know the city (but keep a map as a back-up!). Although the city lacks an efficient public transport system, there are other reliable alternatives, like metered taxi services and car-hire options, should you want to drive yourself around town or get out for a day trip to some of the surrounding areas.

Getting to Cape Town

BY AIR

Cape Town International Airport is operated by the Airports Company of South Africa (ACSA; tel: 086 727 7888; www.airports.co.za). Located along the N2 highway, it takes between 15 and 20 minutes to reach the city centre from the airport outside rush hours.

International airlines that fly daily to Cape Town include:

Air France
Tel: 086 134 0340; www.airfrance.com
British Airways
Tel: 021 936 9000; www.ba.com
Singapore Airlines
Tel: 021 674 0601; www.singaporeair.com
South African Airways
Tel: 021 936 1111; www.flysaa.com

INTERNAL

There are daily flights to Cape Town from Durban, Johannesburg, Bloemfontein and Port Elizabeth with the following airlines:

South African Airways
Tel: 021 936 1111
SA Airlink
Tel: 021 936 1111

BA/Comair
Tel: 021 934 1362
Kulula
Tel: 086 158 5852

BY RAIL

Spoornet's **Shosholoza Meyl** (tel: 021 449 4596/2731; www.spoornet.co.za) offers a daily Trans-Karoo service linking Cape Town to Johannesburg and Pretoria.

For extreme luxury there is the privately owned **Rovos Rail** (tel: 021 421 4020; www.rovos.com) or the famous **Blue Train** (tel: 021 449 2672/2991; www.bluetrain.co.za).

> The roads in the Cape area are excellent. In South Africa you drive on the left-hand side of the road. Speed limits are generally 60–80kph (35–50mph) in towns and up to 120kph (75mph) on national highways.

BY BUS

Greyhound
Tel: 083 915 9000; www.greyhound.co.za
Translux
Tel: 0861 589 282; www.translux.co.za or www.computicket.com
Intercape Mainliner
Tel: 0861 287 287; www.intercape.co.za

The **Baz Bus** (tel: 021 439 2323; www.bazbus.co.za) is a popular hop-on/hop-off option of getting around the country.

Left: hitting the open road.

Left: Cape Town's Metrorail.

BY CAR
To hire a car you will require an international driving licence. Major car-rental companies include:
Avis
Tel: 086 102 1111
Budget
Tel: 021 418 5232
Hertz
Tel: 021 935 4800
For a good deal try **Value Car Hire** (tel: 021 696 2198).

Getting Around

FROM THE AIRPORT
There is no rail or bus service from Cape Town International Airport. **Touch Down Taxis** (tel: 021 919 4659) is the official taxi company for the airport or shuttle services like the **Magic Bus** (tel: 021 505 6300).

Golden Arrow (tel: 0800 656 463; www.gabs.co.za) runs basic bus services within the city and around the Peninsula. Pick up a timetable at their terminus in Strand Street. The open-top **City Sightseeing Bus** (tel: 021 511 1784) links the main places of interest within the City Centre.

> A flight ticket can cost anything from R600 to R2 500 for a return ticket to Johannesburg. Kulula.com (www.kulula.com) and 1 Time (www.1time.co.za) are online-based, low-cost airlines that offer better-value deals on flights.

BY TRAIN
Metrorail (tel: 0800 656 463; www.capemetrorail.co.za) operates between Kalk Bay and Fish Hoek on the False Bay Coast, but its notoriously unreliable with schedules and crime issues. It is strongly advisable to travel first class (Metroplus) to avoid being mugged or pickpocketed, especially at off-peak times when security is less tight. Find the railway station on Adderley and Strand streets.

BY TAXI
Sedan Taxis
These can be hired by telephone or at designated taxi ranks. Ask the driver for a quote before getting in. **Rikki's** (tel: 0861 745 547) operates around Cape Town.

Minibus Taxis
Popular amongst daily commuters and extremely cheap. However, they are often overcrowded and their drivers have a reputation for driving recklessly. Simply flag one down in the street, or go to a designated taxi rank in Adderley Street. Take care when travelling alone.

CYCLING
Daytrippers (tel: 021 511 4766; www.daytrippers.co.za) offers half-day tours on mountain bikes or extended tours around the Cape.

VESPA
To explore the city on the back of a retro Vespa contact **Café Vespa** (tel: 021-426 5042).

Right: the City Sightseeing Bus is a good way to see the city.

Walks and Views

The best way to make the most of Table Mountain and all the surrounding forests and woodland areas is by taking a few hours out of your day for a walk, or if you're fit and adventurous, some climbing. There is no better way to get a bird's-eye view of the city as well as take in all the indigenous Cape flora and fauna on offer. There are a variety of routes and trails to choose from; just be sure you're wearing a good pair of shoes, lather yourself in sunscreen and preferably travel in a group. For details of Cape Town's outdoor options, *see also Parks and Reserves, p.96–101.*

Table Mountain

City Center, also accessible from Southern Suburbs; tel: 021 712 7471; www.sanparks.org; fees for Cape of Good Hope, Boulders and Silvermine; map p.132–9
The quickest way to climb the mountain is to take the **cableway**. Most people take this straight to the top, where they visit the restaurant or bar, have a quick walk around, then take the cable-car down. But it is worth making a half-day or day of it. There are plenty of picnic spots, viewing platforms and a variety of walks, some of which continue down the Peninsula. Whatever you decide, take some warm clothing; it may be sunny and hot down below, but is likely to be quite cold on top. Climbers and hikers have opened over 350 separate routes to the summit of Table Mountain, ranging from easy to very difficult.
SEE ALSO PARKS AND RESERVES, P.96

PIPE TRACK

A popular walk is the Pipe Track, which starts at Kloof Nek, where there's parking, and continues on to Corridor Ravine. It's about 6km (4 miles) one-way, and the return trip takes about five hours. It's mostly (but not always) flat, running along the contours of the mountain, and the views down over the coast of the Atlantic Seaboard to Camps Bay and its surroundings are magical.

Left and right: Table Mountain National Park.

Left: Cape Town from Table Mountain.

A new hiking trail, **Hoerikwaggo**, after the Khoikhoi name for Table Mountain, runs the full length of the Peninsula (tel: 021 465 8515; www.hoerikwaggo.co.za). This five-day hiking trail starts from Deer Park, above Vredehoek. Overnight stops, in huts or tents, are made on the Back Table, then at Silvermine, Red Hill, above Smitswinkel Bay, and finally at the Goldfields Centre near Cape Point.

LION'S HEAD

Another walk, popular with locals early in the morning before they go to work, is to the top of Lion's Head. At 669 metres (2,194ft), the summit takes an hour or so to reach if you're fit, and offers a breathtaking bird's-eye view of the city on all sides. It's a favourite at sunset as well, and during a full moon. Quite steep at the beginning, it then pans out, before ladders and chains embedded in the rock aid the final stretch to the top. There is an alternative route using the contour path. It's a safe walk, usually with lots of walkers on a warm day, and well worth the effort.

PLATTEKLIP GORGE

The climb up Platteklip Gorge is another very popular route for locals and tourists wanting to explore the mountain. The track zigzags to the top of the mountain from Tafelberg Road. It is about 3km (1¾ miles), and takes fit walkers about an hour to complete. If you want to take the cable-car down, turn right at the top (Fountain Peak) and follow the path to Upper Cableway Station.

SKELETON GORGE

Skeleton Gorge is another well-liked Table Mountain climb. Start at the back of Kirstenbosch or along the Contour Path from Rhodes Memorial or from the Newlands Forest. The gorge, which is very steep, was a favourite walk of the South African statesman General Jan Christiaan Smuts, who walked it regularly until he was well into his 70s. It leads through dense, lush forest, then climbs over steep rocky sections to **Maclear's**

Beacon, at 1,086 metres (3,560ft). Erected in 1843 by the astronomer Sir Thomas Maclear, the beacon was part of an experiment to measure the circumference of the earth more accurately. Up here you'll see the **Hely-Hutchinson Dam** (look for the red disas in full bloom in late summer) and the aqueduct leading to it.

ORANGE KLOOF PROTECTED AREA

Encircled by the Constantia Corner Ridge and Bel Ombre, the Back Table and the Twelve Apostles, this area is strictly permit-only. Groups of up to 12 people can organise a free permit and a guide to take them through this splendid wilderness area. Some highlights on this walk include the indigenous forest, yellowwoods, ancient milkwood trees and the kloofs covered in ferns. Other guided walks take visitors to Hell's Gate with its waterfalls and pools, and Disa Gorge, which one can climb to the Back Table of the mountain.

Tourist information and permits can be obtained at the Table Mountain National Park office, tel: 021 701 8692.

CONSTANTIA NEK

This is probably the easiest way up the mountain, ambling leisurely up a jeep-track to the back of Table Mountain. This is the perfect walk for those with sore knees. The trail starts at the car park opposite the Constantia Nek Restaurant (on the Constantia Nek Pass) and can take up to four hours, if you're taking a slow stroll.

Tokai Forest

Southern Suburbs; tel: 021 712 7471; daily 8am–6pm; entrance charge: Braai area R5, R2 per vehicle, free for all walkers

While not really a fully fledged forest, this is a good spot to enjoy a brisk walk and some fresh mountain air. There are usually lots of cyclists on the path, but they're friendly and accommodating as they come past. An interesting variety of trees, birds and small wildlife.

Kirstenbosch National Botanical Gardens

Rhodes Drive, Newlands; tel: 021 799-8783; www.sanbi.org; Sept–May: daily 8am–7pm, June–Aug: daily 8am–6pm; entrance charge

For those wanting a less strenuous walk, this is the best place to start. Meander through the well-manicured gardens looking up at the imposing mountain above you. There are lots of shady spots with garden benches and water-drinking fountains where you can catch your breath and take in the lush scenery. Guided tours can be arranged.

SEE ALSO PARKS AND RESERVES, P.97

Serious Hikes

The walks listed above can easily be done in a day. There are others which can take up to a week. The first overnight trail to be established was the **Cape of Good Hope Hiking Trail**, which takes two days and covers about 33km (20 miles) in all (call the Buffelsfontein Visitor Centre; tel: 021 780 9204 for more information and to book). The first day, which covers about 10.5km (6 miles) of rugged terrain, leads past lonely, windswept beaches on the Atlantic coastline, passes the wreck of the *Phyllisia*, and then follows the eastern boundary of the reserve to overnight huts near Cape Point. Herds of bontebok, eland and other antelope are usually seen grazing along this stretch. The second day, covering 19km (12 miles), concentrates on the Cape of Good Hope and Cape Point.

The overnight huts (World War II observation points of the Coastal Defence Corps) are equipped with toilets, hot showers, bunks and mattresses, gas stoves and *braais*.

SEE ALSO PARKS AND RESERVES, P.97

Walking in the Winelands

Situated less than 20km (12½ miles) inland of False Bay as the crow flies, **Stellenbosch** lies 110 metres (360ft) above sea level, but it is encircled by several impressive mountain ranges. Notable amongst these are the **Groot Drakenstein** (Large Dragon's Rock), **Stellenbosch Mountains**, **Simonsberg** and **Helderberg** (Clear Mountain). While they all provide a picturesque backdrop to the Winelands, they're also characterised by the wealth of proteas and wild flowers. If you're up for a walk, there is a relatively easy circular 6km (4-mile) **Swartboskloof–Sosyskloof Trail** through the **Jonkershoek Nature Reserve**. For something a little more challenging, try the Vineyard Trail connecting the **Papegaaiberg** (Parrot Mountain) to the **Kuils River**. Overnight hikes can be taken through the **Hottentots Holland Nature Reserve**; the entrance lies off the R321 between Grabouw and Villiersdorp.

SEE ALSO PARKS AND RESERVES, P.97

Other guided hikes take visitors to remote and beautiful spots such as Hell's Gate, with its tumbling waterfalls and pools, and Disa Gorge, up which one can ascend to the Back Table. Contact the Table Mountain National Park for information and permits.

Safety

It is extremely important to stock up on ample water, comfortable shoes, a hat, sunscreen, mobile phone and a warm top or light rain jacket before you set out on any mountain walk. Never hike alone (even the paths are monitored by mountain police), and always inform someone of your whereabouts. If you go hiking, it is important to be security-conscious. Always stick to the paths and trails, and if the mist comes down, stay where you are rather than try to make your way down, which can be very dangerous. In case of emergency, take these numbers with you: **Police**, tel: 10111, and **Mountain Rescue Service**, tel: 021 948 9900.

Right: the Winelands have plenty of trails for exploring.

Atlas

The following streetplan of Cape Town makes it easy to find the attractions listed in our A–Z section. A selective index to streets and sights will help you find other locations throughout the city

Map Legend

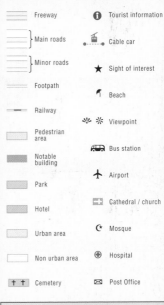

Freeway	Tourist information
Main roads	Cable car
Minor roads	Sight of interest
Footpath	Beach
Railway	Viewpoint
Pedestrian area	Bus station
Notable building	Airport
Park	Cathedral / church
Hotel	Mosque
Urban area	Hospital
Non urban area	Post Office
Cemetery	

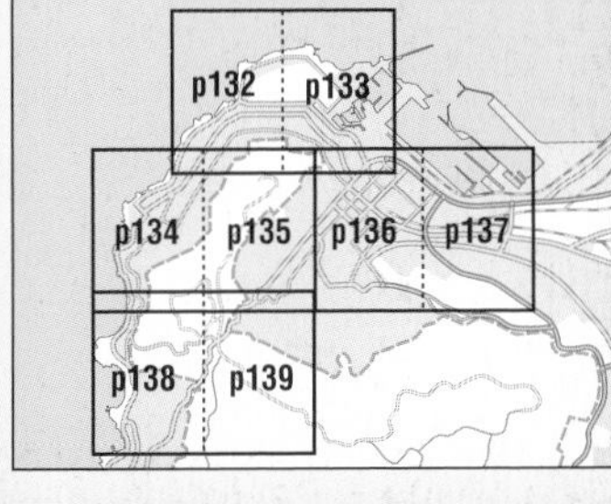

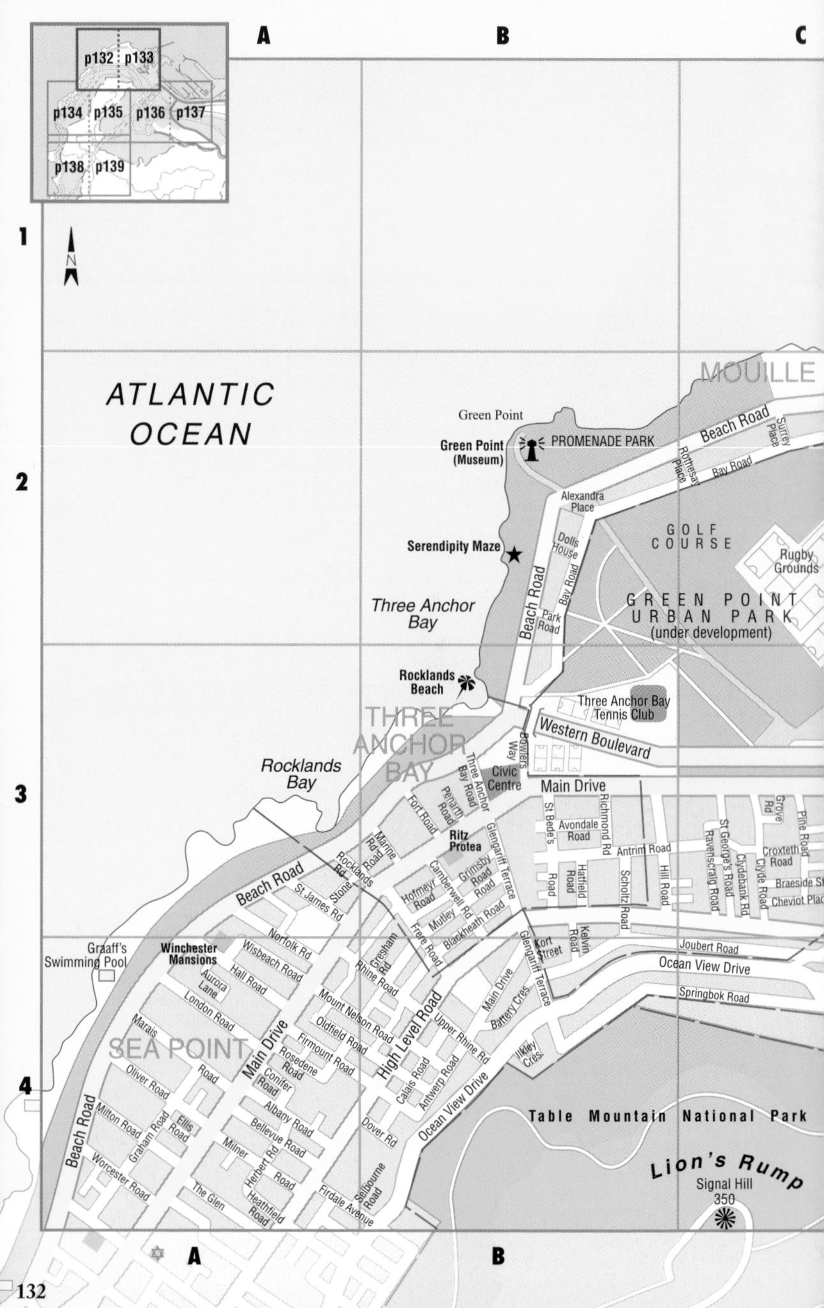

A
B
C
1
2
3
4
p132
p133
p134
p135
p136
p137
p138
p139
N
ATLANTIC OCEAN
MOUILLE
Green Point
Green Point (Museum)
PROMENADE PARK
Beach Road
Surrey Place
Rothesay Place
Bay Road
Alexandra Place
GOLF COURSE
Serendipity Maze
Dolls House
Rugby Grounds
Three Anchor Bay
GREEN POINT URBAN PARK (under development)
Park Road
Rocklands Beach
THREE ANCHOR BAY
Three Anchor Bay Tennis Club
Western Boulevard
Bowlers Way
Rocklands Bay
Civic Centre
Main Drive
Penarth Road
Fort Road
Ritz Protea
Avondale Road
Richmond Rd
St Bede's Road
Antrim Road
Hill Road
Scholtz Road
Hatfield Road
Glengariff Terrace
Kelvin Road
Kort Street
Joubert Road
Ocean View Drive
Springbok Road
St George's Road
Ravenscraig Road
Clydebank Road
Clyde Road
Grove Rd
Pine Road
Croxteth Road
Braeside St
Cheviot Place
Marine Road
Rocklands Rd
Stone
St James Rd
Hofmeyr Road
Camberwell Rd
Grimsby Road
Mutley
Blackheath Road
Frere Road
Gresham Rd
Rhine Road
Norfolk Rd
Wisbeach Road
Hall Road
Graaff's Swimming Pool
Winchester Mansions
Aurora Lane
London Road
Mount Nelson Road
Oldfield Road
Firmount Road
High Level Road
Upper Rhine Rd
Main Drive
Battery Cres.
Ilkley Cres.
SEA POINT
Marais Road
Rosedene Road
Conifer Road
Calais Road
Antwerp Road
Oliver Road
Beach Road
Milton Road
Graham Road
Ellis Road
Albany Road
Bellevue Road
Milner Road
Herbert Rd
Dover Rd
Table Mountain National Park
Lion's Rump
Signal Hill
350
Worcester Road
The Glen
Heathfield Road
Firdale Avenue
Sellbourne Road

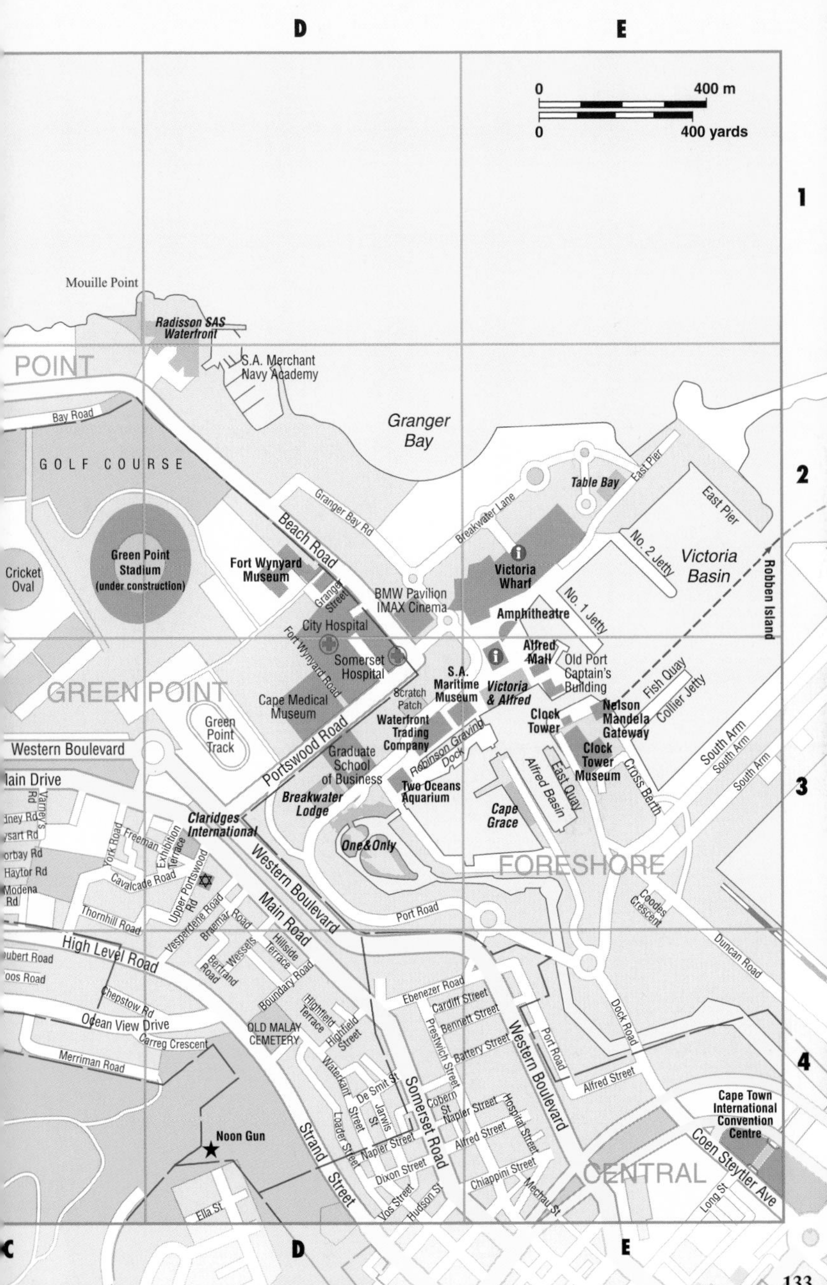
D
E
0
400 m
0
400 yards
1
2
3
4
Mouille Point
Radisson SAS Waterfront
POINT
S.A. Merchant Navy Academy
Granger Bay
Bay Road
GOLF COURSE
Granger Bay Rd
Breakwater Lane
Table Bay
East Pier
East Pier
Beach Road
No. 2 Jetty
Victoria Basin
Robben Island
Cricket Oval
Green Point Stadium (under construction)
Fort Wynyard Museum
Granger Street
BMW Pavilion IMAX Cinema
Victoria Wharf
Amphitheatre
No. 1 Jetty
City Hospital
Fort Wynyard Road
Somerset Hospital
Alfred Mall
Old Port Captain's Building
GREEN POINT
Cape Medical Museum
Scratch Patch
S.A. Maritime Museum
Victoria & Alfred
Fish Quay
Collier Jetty
Green Point Track
Portswood Road
Waterfront Trading Company
Clock Tower
Nelson Mandela Gateway
Western Boulevard
Robinson Graving Dock
Graduate School of Business
Clock Tower Museum
Alfred Basin
East Quay
Cross Berth
South Arm
South Arm
South Arm
Main Drive
Varney's Rd
Breakwater Lodge
Two Oceans Aquarium
Cape Grace
Claridges International
York Road
Freeman
Exhibition Terrace
One&Only
Upper Portswood Rd
Western Boulevard
FORESHORE
Haytor Rd
Modena Rd
Cavalcade Road
Vesperdene Road
Braemar Road
Main Road
Coodes Crescent
Thornhill Road
Port Road
Duncan Road
High Level Road
Bertrand Road
Wessels
Hillside Terrace
Boundary Road
Chepstow Rd
Ebenezer Road
Cardiff Street
Bennett Street
Dock Road
Ocean View Drive
Carreg Crescent
OLD MALAY CEMETERY
Highfield Terrace
Highfield Street
Prestwich Street
Battery Street
Western Boulevard
Port Road
Merriman Road
Waterkant Street
De Smit St
Jarvis St
Somerset Road
Cobern St
Alfred Street
Cape Town International Convention Centre
Noon Gun
Loader Street
Napier Street
Alfred Street
Hospital Street
Coen Steytler Ave
Strand Street
Napier Street
Dixon Street
Chiappini Street
CENTRAL
Vos Street
Hudson St
Mechau St
Long St
Ella St
C
D
E

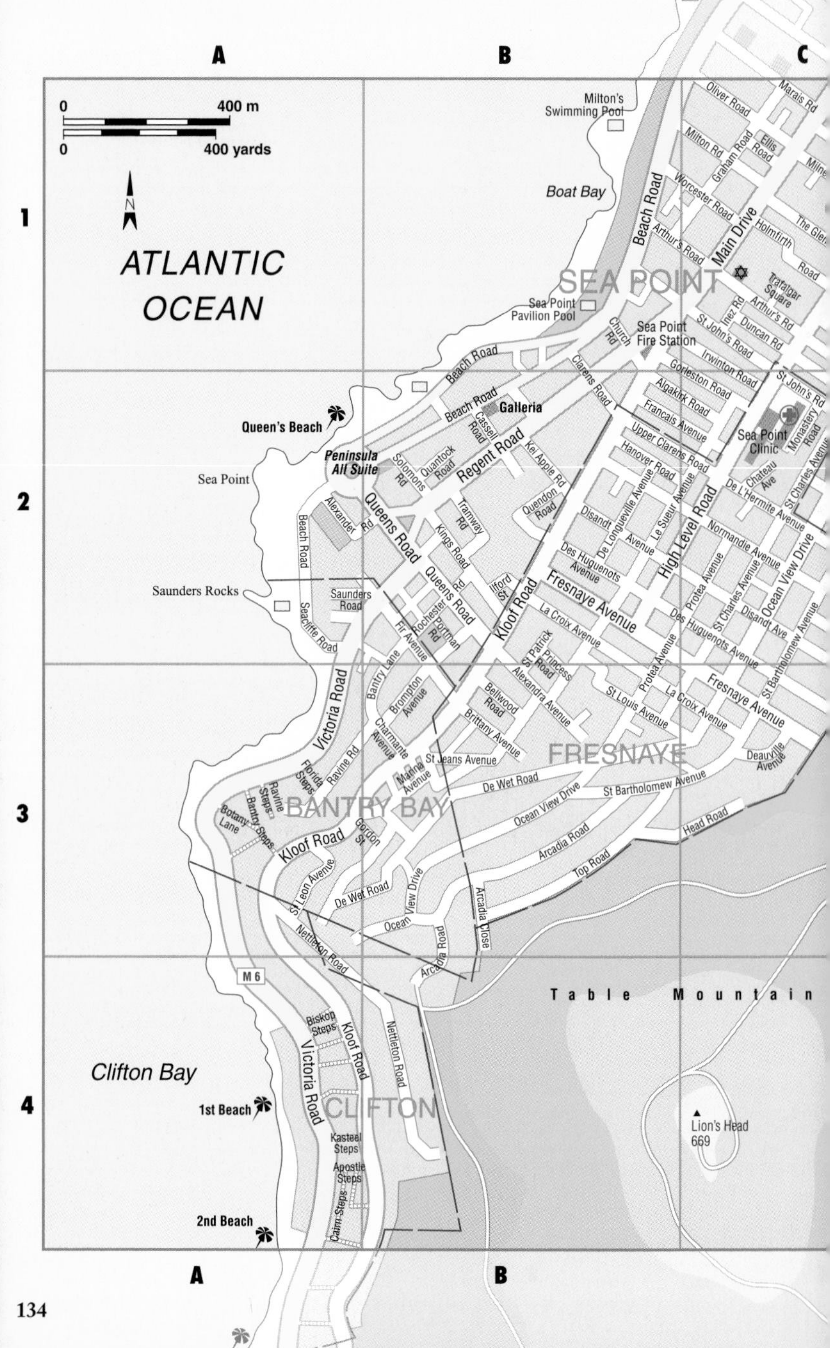

A
B
C
1
2
3
4
0
400 m
0
400 yards
N
ATLANTIC OCEAN
Milton's Swimming Pool
Boat Bay
Beach Road
SEA POINT
Sea Point Pavilion Pool
Sea Point Fire Station
Queen's Beach
Galleria
Peninsula All Suite
Sea Point
Saunders Rocks
Sea Point Clinic
FRESNAYE
BANTRY BAY
Table Mountain
M 6
Clifton Bay
1st Beach
CLIFTON
2nd Beach
Lion's Head 669
Queens Road
Regent Road
Kloof Road
Fresnaye Avenue
High Level Road
Main Drive
Victoria Road
Ocean View Drive
Nettleton Road
De Wet Road
Arcadia Road
Top Road
Head Road
St Bartholomew Avenue

Table Mountain National Park
Signal Hill 350
Lion's Rump
Signal Hill Road
SCHOTSCHE KLOOF
St Mary Maternity
TAMBOERSKLOOF
Fresnaye Sports Club
Conradie Recreation Ground
Mount Nelson
GARDENS
Volks Hospital
DE WAAL PARK
Leeuwenhof & Bo-Tuin
New Church Street
Kloof Nek Road
Kloof Street
Camp Street
Military Road
Ocean View Drive
High Level Road
Quarry Hill
M 62
p132 p133
p134 p135 p136 p137
p138 p139
D
E
C
1
2
3
4

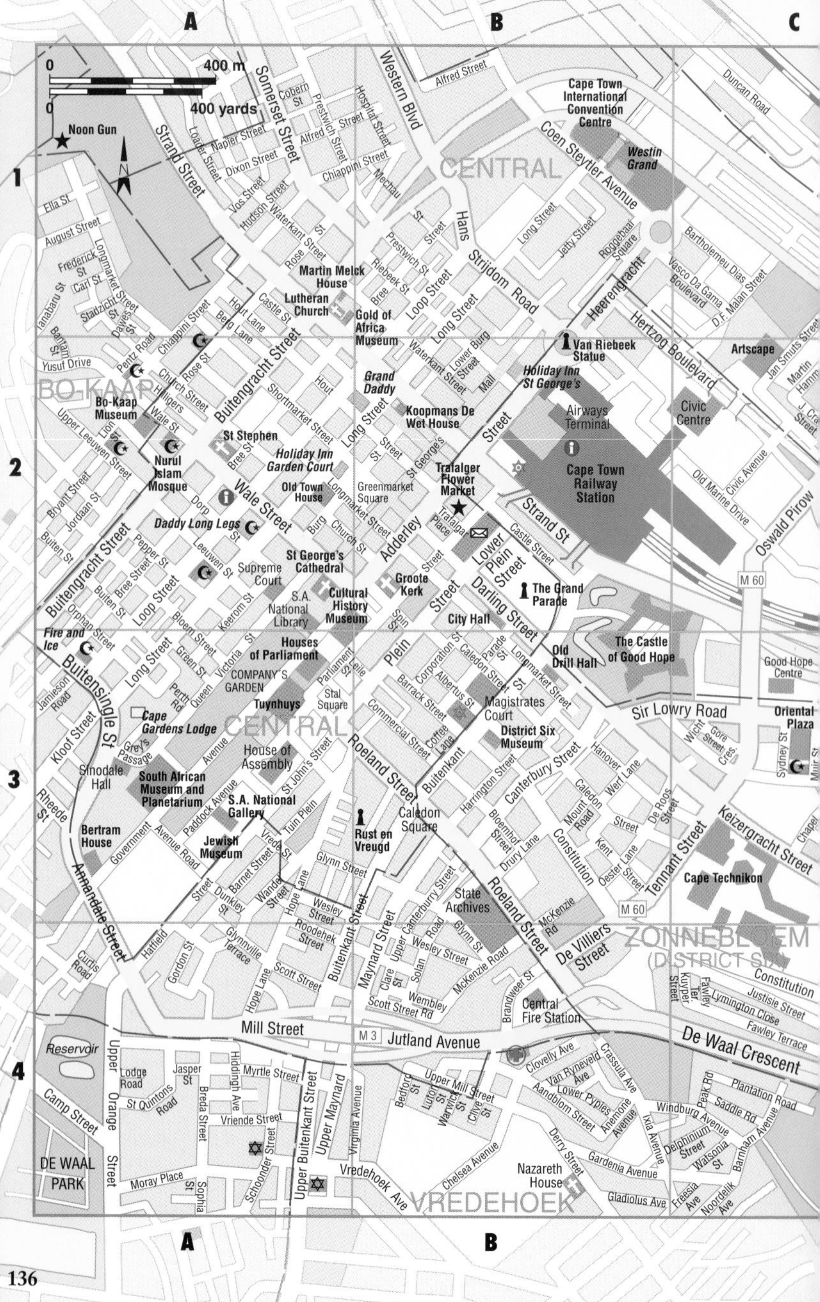
A
B
C
1
2
3
4
0
400 m
400 yards
Noon Gun
CENTRAL
BO-KAAP
CENTRAL
ZONNEBLOEM
(DISTRICT SIX)
VREDEHOEK
Cape Town International Convention Centre
Westin Grand
Martin Melck House
Lutheran Church
Gold of Africa Museum
Van Riebeek Statue
Artscape
Holiday Inn St George's
Grand Daddy
Koopmans De Wet House
Airways Terminal
Civic Centre
Bo-Kaap Museum
St Stephen
Holiday Inn Garden Court
Trafalger Flower Market
Cape Town Railway Station
Nurul Islam Mosque
Old Town House
Greenmarket Square
Daddy Long Legs
St George's Cathedral
Supreme Court
Groote Kerk
The Grand Parade
S.A. National Library
Cultural History Museum
City Hall
Fire and Ice
Houses of Parliament
Old Drill Hall
The Castle of Good Hope
Good Hope Centre
COMPANY'S GARDEN
Stal Square
Magistrates Court
Oriental Plaza
Cape Gardens Lodge
Tuynhuys
District Six Museum
Grey's Passage
House of Assembly
Sinodale Hall
South African Museum and Planetarium
S.A. National Gallery
Caledon Square
Bertram House
Jewish Museum
Rust en Vreugd
Cape Technikon
State Archives
Central Fire Station
Reservoir
DE WAAL PARK
Nazareth House
Strand Street
Somerset Street
Western Blvd
Alfred Street
Duncan Road
Coen Steytler Avenue
Hans Strijdom Road
Heerengracht
Hertzog Boulevard
Buitengracht Street
Wale Street
Long Street
Loop Street
Adderley Street
Strand St
Darling Street
Plein Street
Sir Lowry Road
Roeland Street
Buitensingle St
Kloof Street
Annandale Street
Keizergracht Street
Tennant Street
De Villiers Street
Constitution Street
Mill Street
M 3
Jutland Avenue
De Waal Crescent
M 60
Upper Orange Street
Camp Street
Upper Buitenkant Street
Upper Maynard
Vredehoek Ave
Oswald Pirow
Civic Avenue
Old Marine Drive

D
E
Duncan Dock
Tanker Basin
Ben Schoeman Dock
Mole
Jackson Wharf
Repair Quay
Customs Gate
Duncan Road
Elliot Basin
Ocean
Vanguard
Sturrock Dock
Alkmaar Road
Berrio Road
Small Craft Harbour
Royal Cape Yacht Club
Malan House
Table Bay Boulevard
Woodstock
FORESHORE
Esplanade
Tide Street
Beach Road
Lower Church Street
New Market Street
Albert Road
Sir Lowry Road
Victoria Road
TRAFALGAR PARK
Eastern Boulevard
Keizergracht Street
Searle Street
Woodstock Hospital
Holiday Inn
Coronation Road
Chester Street
Eden Road
Cambridge Street
Beresford Road
Premier Road
Christiaan Street
Constitution
Perth Street
DEVILS PEAK ESTATE
p132 p133
p134 p135 p136 p137
p138 p139
1
2
3
4
C
D
E

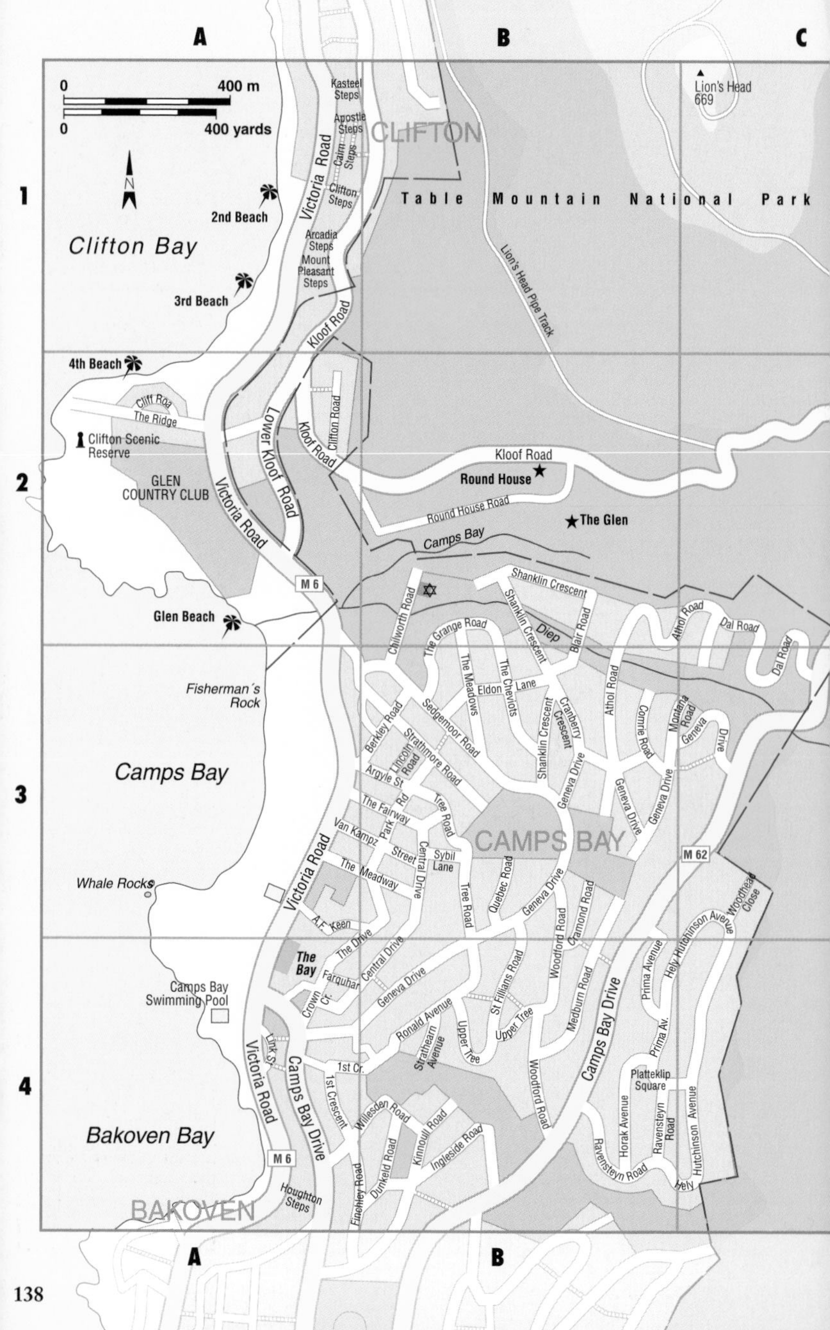

A
B
C
1
2
3
4
0
400 m
0
400 yards
N
Kasteel Steps
Apostle Steps
Cairn Steps
Clifton Steps
Arcadia Steps
Mount Pleasant Steps
CLIFTON
Lion's Head 669
Table Mountain National Park
Victoria Road
2nd Beach
Clifton Bay
3rd Beach
Lion's Head Pipe Track
Kloof Road
4th Beach
Cliff Road
The Ridge
Clifton Scenic Reserve
GLEN COUNTRY CLUB
Lower Kloof Road
Clifton Road
Round House
Round House Road
The Glen
Camps Bay
M 6
Glen Beach
Shanklin Crescent
Chilworth Road
The Grange Road
Blair Road
Diep
Athol Road
Dal Road
The Meadows
The Cheviots
Eldon Lane
Fisherman's Rock
Berkley Road
Sedgemoor Road
Strathmore Road
Lincoln Road
Cranberry Crescent
Comrie Road
Montana Road
Geneva Drive
Argyle St
The Fairway
Park Rd
Tree Road
Van Kampz Street
Sybil Lane
Central Drive
CAMPS BAY
M 62
The Meadway
Quebec Road
Camps Bay
Whale Rocks
A.F. Keen
The Drive
Woodford Road
Ormond Road
Woodhead Close
Hely Hutchinson Avenue
Prima Avenue
The Bay
Farquhar
Crown Cr.
St Fillians Road
Medburn Road
Camps Bay Drive
Camps Bay Swimming Pool
Ronald Avenue
Upper Tree
Prima Av.
Link St
1st Cr.
Strathearn Avenue
Platteklip Square
1st Crescent
Willesden Road
Kinnoull Road
Horak Avenue
Ravensteyn Road
Hutchinson Avenue
Bakoven Bay
Ingleside Road
Dunkeld Road
Finchley Road
Houghton Steps
Hely
BAKOVEN

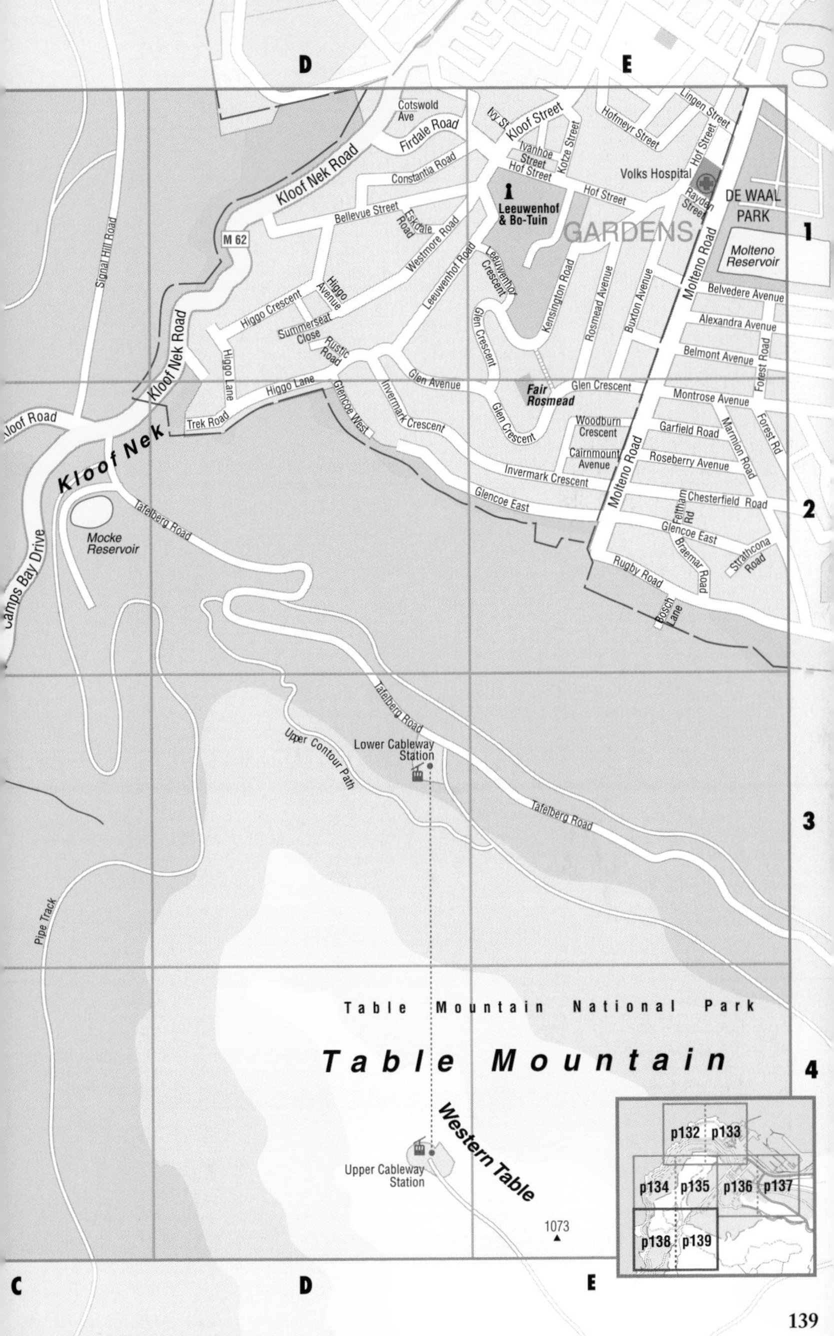

D
E
Cotswold Ave
Firdale Road
Kloof Nek Road
Ivy St
Kloof Street
Lingen Street
Hofmeyr Street
Ivanhoe Street
Kotze Street
Hof Street
Constantia Road
Volks Hospital
Hof Street
Leeuwenhof & Bo-Tuin
Rayden Street
DE WAAL PARK
Bellevue Street
Eskdale Road
GARDENS
Molteno Reservoir
M 62
Westmore Road
Leeuwenhof Road
Leeuwenhof Crescent
Molteno Road
Signal Hill Road
Higgo Avenue
Higgo Crescent
Kensington Road
Rosmead Avenue
Buxton Avenue
Belvedere Avenue
Alexandra Avenue
Summerseat Close
Glen Crescent
Belmont Avenue
Forest Road
Rustic Road
Kloof Nek Road
Higgo Lane
Glen Avenue
Higgo Lane
Glen Crescent
Fair Rosmead
Montrose Avenue
Kloof Road
Trek Road
Glencoe West
Invermark Crescent
Glen Crescent
Woodburn Crescent
Garfield Road
Forest Rd
Kloof Nek
Cairnmount Avenue
Roseberry Avenue
Marmion Road
Invermark Crescent
Molteno Road
Glencoe East
Feltham Rd
Chesterfield Road
Tafelberg Road
Mocke Reservoir
Glencoe East
Braemar Road
Strathcona Road
Camps Bay Drive
Rugby Road
Bosch Lane
Tafelberg Road
Lower Cableway Station
Upper Contour Path
Tafelberg Road
Pipe Track
Table Mountain National Park
Table Mountain
Western Table
Upper Cableway Station
1073
p132
p133
p134
p135
p136
p137
p138
p139
1
2
3
4
C
D
E

Street Atlas Index

PLACES OF INTEREST

STREETS

Index

T

U–V

W–X

Insight Smart Guide: Cape Town
Written by: Sally Munro
Edited by: Jason Mitchell, Joanna Potts
Proofread and indexed by: Neil Titman
Photography by: All Pictures APA/Alex Havret except: Bang Bang club 90/91, 90BL, 91BR; Cellars Hohenort 34; Foresters Arms 35; Marine Hermanus 68, 69; Fiction Bar 92B, 93B; Foto Libra 8; Getty 60BR; Getty 62BR&BL; Jazzart Dance Theatre 86/87; Karma Lounge 92; Leonardo 63B, 64B, 65, 66, 66B, 69B, 94/95; On Broadway 89B; Mary Evans 60; Media Club SouthAfrica 88, 89T; South African Tourism 9; Superstock 9C; The Assembly 90C; Topham 61TL; Tri-Continental Film Festival 52/53
Cover picture by: 4Corners Images
Picture Manager: Steven Lawrence
Maps: Mapping Ideas Ltd
Series Editor: Jason Mitchell
First Edition 2009

Printed in Singapore by Insight Print Services (Pte) Ltd
Worldwide distribution enquiries:
Apa Publications GmbH & Co. Verlag KG (Singapore Branch) 38 Joo Koon Road, Singapore 628990; tel: (65) 6865 1600; fax: (65) 6861 6438
Distributed in the UK and Ireland by:
GeoCenter International Ltd
Meridian House, Churchill Way West, Basingstoke, Hampshire RG21 6YR; tel: (44 1256) 817 987; fax: (44 1256) 817 988
Distributed in the United States by:
Langenscheidt Publishers, Inc.
36–36 33rd Street 4th Floor, Long Island City, New York 11106; tel: (1 718) 784 0055; fax: (1 718) 784 0640l
Contacting the Editors
We would appreciate it if readers would alert us to errors or outdated information by writing to:
Apa Publications, PO Box 7910, London SE1 1WE, UK; fax: (44 20) 7403 0290;
e-mail: insight@apaguide.co.uk